A Year of
Miracles

ALSO BY MARIANNE WILLIAMSON

A Return to Love

A Woman's Worth

Illuminata

Emma & Mommy Talk to God

Healing the Soul of America

Illuminated Prayers

Enchanted Love

Everyday Grace

The Gift of Change

The Age of Miracles

A Course in Weight Loss

The Law of Divine Compensation

A Year of
Miracles

DAILY DEVOTIONS AND
REFLECTIONS

Marianne Williamson

HarperOne
An Imprint of HarperCollinsPublishers

HarperOne

HarperCollins books may be purchased for educational, business, or sales promotional use. For information, please e-mail the Special Markets Department at SPsales@harpercollins.com.

HarperCollins website: http://www.harpercollins.com

FIRST HARPERCOLLINS PAPERBACK EDITION PUBLISHED IN 2015

Designed by Ralph Fowler

ISBN 978–0–06–220551–3

Library of Congress Cataloging-in-Publication Data

Williamson, Marianne.
   A year of miracles : daily devotions and reflections / Marianne Williamson.
      pages cm
   ISBN 978–0–06–220550–6 (hardcover)
   1. Religious life. 2. Spiritual life. 3. Miracles—Miscellanea. I. Title.
BL624.W5755   2013
204'.32—dc23   2013044249

15 16 17 18 19   RRD(H)   10 9 8 7 6 5 4 3 2 1

INTRODUCTION

A miracle is a shift in thinking, a shift from fear to love. At first glance, that sounds a bit ridiculous. How does shifting a thought cause a miraculous change?

And yet it does exactly that. For every thought we think creates *form* on some level. A simple thought—seemingly trivial or even unimportant—carries within it the power to move mountains. And that is the least it can do. There is no worldly power—no money, no technology, no business or government—that can match in power the power we wield by simply using our minds for the purposes of love.

"I love, I love!" you might say. And of course you love. We all do. The problem, however, is that we do not love only. We love, but then we take it back. We love, but then we stop when it becomes inconvenient. We love, but only until the ego is challenged by the thought of risk.

And so it is that while we love, we do not wield the power of love. We love, but we do not work miracles.

The purpose of this book is to help guide your thinking to the thoughts of love that will break the chains of fear that bind you. One moment, one situation, one thought at a time, we can evolve beyond the lower thought forms that keep us bound. And in so doing, we become miracle-workers, working miracles for ourselves and for all the world.

....

The first place to start working miracles is not in the world around you, but in yourself. You're not going to work a miracle in your environment, but in your mind.

Because mind is Cause and the world is Effect, we change the world by changing the thoughts we think about the world.

Begin with a simple step:

Put down this book and look around you. Look at the chair you're sitting on, or the table that's next to you, or the walls around you. And ask yourself this: *What are my thoughts about this chair, or this table, or this wall? That they're not good enough, or nice enough? Or do I never really think about them all, just taking them for granted?*

Now try a simple shift: *Wow, how lucky I am to have a chair. Billions of people do not. How fortunate I am to have a table. Billions of people do not. And how lucky I am to have walls around me. Billions of people do not.*

Notice the slight energetic shift that occurred within you when you made that change, how your thinking went from a kind of hard place to someplace softer, from somewhere floating around your head to someplace deep within your heart.

And now know this: YOU JUST SHIFTED THE UNIVERSE.

Yes, that is what I said.

The wind currents at the North Pole are affected when a butterfly flaps its wings in South America, and the entire world is affected by every thought you think. You don't have to believe this idea, of course. A miracle-worker simply knows it.

Anyone can be a miracle-worker—anyone who chooses to be. Anyone can hear the sound of an ancient melody that calls to all of us, beckoning us to remember who we truly are and what power we have. A miracle-worker accepts the idea that every thought has an effect not only on the one who thinks it but on everyone else as well.

It isn't necessary to believe any of this. This is a guidebook, not a doctrine. Simply try it out. And watch things change.

....

So we've already established that you might not have had a clue about the significance of your chair, or your table, or your wall. And yet the meaning that we ascribe to anything will determine what meaning it ultimately has for us. Think something isn't good enough, and it never will be. Think something is wonderful, and it will only get better.

So thoughts like this are miraculous thoughts:

> *I give thanks for this chair, for this table, for this wall.*

> *I remember with compassion those who do not have such simple amenities, and I pray they will receive what they need.*

> *I surrender myself, that I might be used in bringing the end of suffering to all the world.*

Now what did such thoughts just do for you? Not for others, but for you?

They established you within a different corner of the universe. You moved from someone with a slightly open heart to someone with a more fully opened heart. *And the more open your heart, the more miracles you'll receive.*

For miracles occur naturally as expressions of love. When you choose to love, you choose to work miracles.

What follows are 365 readings that, when read daily, encourage you to stay focused on love and to avoid the distractions of fear, anxiety, shame, guilt, and everything else that is not built on love. It is this daily choice to think with love that determines what miracles come into our lives. The universe is ready to bless you. Are you ready to receive these gifts? My prayer is that this book will help you.

A Year of
Miracles

DAY 1

The universe is conspiring in every moment to bring me happiness and peace.

The universe is not random but intentional. It reflects the will of God, the cosmic Thought driving all things toward greater perfection.

My ego mind—my own self-hatred masquerading as self-love—would point me always in the direction of fear, luring me toward the blaming thought, the attack or defense, the perception of guilt in myself or others. Its goal is my suffering, or the hell of my own illusions.

The spirit within leads only to joy, as it inspires me to see the love in everyone and the possibility of miracles that lie inherent in all things. The universe itself is the handwriting of God, as He constantly creates and re-creates the perfection that He is. Within that perfection I have my true being, and within my true being I am happy and at peace.

Today I will not be tempted to wander the byroads of pain, but rather I will set my feet upon the path of joy and peace. May the Spirit of God protect my mind from any forces of fear that would divert my thinking. May I not be deceived into a false belief in the validity of guilt and attack, but rather may I be constantly uplifted to the divine perceptions of innocence and love. For there shall I experience the bliss of God's creation. Now and always. Amen.

DAY 2

Forgiveness sets me free of pain.

We don't forgive someone for their sake; we forgive them for the sake of our own peace of mind. Any attack on another person is an attack upon ourselves, for in the spiritual universe there is only one of us here. What I think about anyone else I'm thinking about myself. All of us are joined in the oneness of God's love. Only love is real and only love has power; everything else is a mortal illusion.

Forgiveness is my salvation from pain. If I believe in the reality of what "you did to me," then I will feel as though the consequences of what you did to me are real. By "overlooking," I will "overcome." The question becomes this: Where do I put my faith? Do I put my faith in something loveless that someone did to me, or in the eternal love that lies beyond and corrects all things? To the extent that I withdraw my attachment to what you did, I will no longer be affected by what you did. I have decided to put my faith elsewhere. That is the miracle of forgiveness.

Something loveless might have occurred in my life, and of course I have to process my feelings . . . but I don't have to indulge them. I need to honor my feelings . . . but I don't have to spew them. By standing on the spiritual truth that only love is real, I develop the ability to endure the gap in time between the pain of someone having hurt me, and the miracle of my release from suffering. In time, as forgiveness becomes my way of life, the gap itself will no longer exist.

DAY 3

There can be no darkness
where I provide the light.

Light is to darkness what love is to fear; in the presence of one, the other disappears. All the darkness in my life—the fears, neuroses, dysfunctions, and diseases—are not so much things as the absence of things. They represent not the presence of a problem but rather the absence of the answer. And the answer is love. All fearful manifestations disappear in the presence of love.

Today I make a stand against darkness, knowing that love will save me from the painful delusions that occupy my mind. As I surrender my mind to love, and dedicate myself to the Light of True Being, then love will cast out my fears and light will cast out all darkness.

It is not the love given to me by others, but only the love that I myself provide, that will save me today from suffering. I call to mind any person from whom I have been withholding love or forgiveness, or situation from which I have been withholding faith in miracles, and surrender such thoughts for healing.

God goes with me everywhere, because God is in my mind.

God is not outside me, but lives within my heart. He lives in my mind, as I live in His. There is nothing I can do, and nowhere I can go, that can separate me from God.

Believing in a separation between myself and God is at the core of all my problems. For no such separation exists. I am not alone, for God is always with me.

There is no problem that God cannot solve. He guides me to right thought and action whenever I request it. He parts all waters and calms all storms, through His spirit that lives within me.

No matter what I go through today, I need not fear. For God is all-powerful and God is here. I am never separate from the One who created me. There is nothing I can do to make Him turn his face away from me. I am loved, I am cared for, and I am totally safe in the arms of God.

DAY 5

On the Miracle of Surrender

God knows our crooked places that need to be made straight, the wounds in our hearts that fester for years unhealed, the broken pieces of our lives that seem beyond repair. And He who is the author of miracles has infinite desire as well as power to heal them all.

At a certain point, it doesn't really matter so much how we got to be a certain way. Until we *admit* our character defects—and take responsibility for the fact that regardless of where we got them, *they are ours now*—they will not go away. For God Himself will not violate our free will. We can talk to a therapist for hours about how our relationship with Mom or Dad made us develop a certain behavioral characteristic, but that of itself will not make it go away. Naming it, surrendering it to God, and asking Him to remove it—*that's* the miracle of personal transformation. It won't go away in a moment, necessarily, but its days are numbered. The medicine is in your psychic bloodstream.

In the spiritual universe only love is real, and nothing else exists.

While the appearances of the three-dimensional world would deceive me into the false belief that there are powers more powerful than the will of God, in fact only love is the kingdom, the power, and the glory. My physical senses are useful tools, but they are not the arbiters of ultimate truth. Only the love in my heart is the knower of all things.

The world has trained me to believe in the illusions of fear and separation, and to disbelieve in the truth that lies beyond them. Today I make a stand for truth, as I extend my perceptions beyond what my senses reveal to me, to what I know to be true in my heart. I commit to the realization that only love is real, and I recognize the ultimate nonexistence of anything else. This way I gain the power of a miracle-worker, a channel for God in His will that only love prevail.

No matter what situation I am in today, I will remember that only love is real. I will not be waylaid by false appearances. When I cannot find my way to true vision, I pray to be reminded that false appearances are powerless before the will of God. I pray that my inner eye be opened to the love within all things.

We cannot save the world without God's help, but He can't save the world without ours. We need His love; He needs our hands and feet. Today I give Him mine.

A love that hovers above the earth, however well intentioned, is not enough to save the world. It is a willing heart and love embodied that carry with them the miraculous authority to turn darkness into light.

God cannot do for us what He cannot do through us, and today I pray that He works through me. May I be used for a higher purpose, as I surrender to Him my hands and feet, my thoughts and behavior. May they reflect His love. May angels guide me, that I might do the part assigned me to help heal the world.

Today is a day of surrender, as I seek not my own goals but the one goal of God. May my heart be so open and my soul so soft that I am a conduit for all things good. May it be revealed to me where to go, what to do, what to say and to whom, that I might serve Him best. In every moment may I remember to pray, "Dear God, please use me." For thus it will be so.

The universe knows how to organize itself. Today I stand back and let it come to me.

Divine organization is inherent in all things. The larger plan is not mine to know and not mine to create; it is simply mine to follow. As a cell contains a natural intelligence by which it fosters the healthy functioning of the body, I too have natural intelligence that fosters the perfect unfolding of my life. My natural intelligence is love, and as long as I cleave to that and that only, all things good and true and peaceful will find their way to me.

I cannot use my fingers to create a design out of a pile of iron shavings; I can only do that by using a magnet. That magnet is the love within me, attracting naturally the most positive events for myself and those around me. Today I will not walk ahead of love. Rather, I will trust that as I rest content within my heart, the universe will automatically find a way to lift me up and bring me peace.

Today I align myself with the will of a loving universe.

The universe is not random but intentional; as a reflection of divine Mind, it intends love and happiness for all living things. The question I want to ask myself in any situation is, "Am I aligned with the will of the universe?"

If I am only seeking my own goals; if I am blaming anyone or living in the past; if I am competing but not collaborating—then I am not aligned with a loving universe. I choose instead a miraculous path. I enter every situation with only one intention: to be a vessel of love and a blessing on my surroundings. May all people who I meet or even think of receive my love.

I needn't worry whether the universe intends my greater good, for it intends a greater good for all living things. The divine weaver is always weaving. I am a thread in the eternal tapestry of God's golden creation, no more or less than anyone else. My accepting this allows me to relax into a consistent knowing that I am blessed. I shall feel this blessing as I choose to bless others.

REFLECTION

On Becoming Who You Are

Wherever you've been, and whatever you've done so far, your entire life was building up to this moment. Now is the time to burst forth into your greatness, a greatness you could never have achieved without going through exactly the things you've gone through. Everything you've experienced was grist for the mill by which you have become who you are. As low as you might have descended, in God there are no limits to how high you can go now. It is not too late. You are not too damaged. In fact, you are better than you know.

Today I choose happiness.

The circumstances of my life may go up and down, for the mortal world is changeable. The immortal world, however, is changeless, for there there is only love. I build my house on the rock of the immortal world. Today I choose only immortal thoughts.

I extend my perception beyond what my senses perceive, to what my heart knows is true. I withdraw my belief that I need anyone or anything to be other than what they are, in order for me to be secure. I know that whenever fear expresses itself, love will ultimately prevail. Therefore I need not fear, nor cry, nor despair. To the extent to which I see what is truly true, I see only cause for happiness.

Happiness is the choice I make today. It does not rest on my circumstances, but on my frame of mind. I surrender to God any emotional habits that lead me down the path of unhappiness, and pray for guidance in shifting my thoughts. In cultivating the habits of happiness, I attract the people and situations that match its frequency. I smile more often, give praise more often, give thanks more often, and am glad more often. For such is my choice today.

I surrender my fears and burdens to God.

I needn't carry into my day the burdens of my existence. Rather, I surrender them into the hands of God. I know that they will be lifted from me, for what I place on the altar in my mind is then altered in my life.

When I do not know what to say or do, He who is alive within me will illumine my thinking and guide my words. When a possible outcome makes me weak with fear, I will feel His arms around me. And when the road seems lonely and long before me, I will know I am not alone.

Dear God,

Please take from me the burdens that I carry.
Please uplift my thinking and bring forth a miracle.
Send a wave of love to disperse my fear.
And so it is.

Amen.

Today I atone for
the mistakes of my past.

While I have made mistakes, I remember today that God is infinitely merciful. I am willing to atone for my errors and make appropriate amends, that the mercy of God be shown to me. I pray for forgiveness, that my heart might be free of shame and guilt. I know that I am a perfect child of God, and that my mistakes do not make me less so.

God sees me not as someone whose guilt calls for punishment, but as someone whose errors call for correction. As I turn to Him and admit my errors, genuinely atoning in my heart for any damage I may have caused to others or to myself, the miraculous power of the Atonement is released on my behalf. I will be given a chance to begin again; as many times as I may have fallen, such is the number of times He lifts me up. For such is the awesome mercy of God.

I atone in my heart for the mistakes I have made: the reckless-ness and irresponsibility, the laziness and dishonesty, the harm I have caused to myself or others. I pray for those who I may have hurt, and ask that they be healed of any pain I might have caused them. I vow to be a better person now, that I might rise where before I had fallen, and shine where I had dwelled in darkness.

The holiness of the present delivers me from the pain of yesterday.

Every moment reveals God's infinite love. Living in the present, I am safe and free. Nothing can keep me bound to the past except my thoughts that would keep me there.

I forgive myself, and others, for any mistakes we made before this moment. I choose not to drag the burden of my past into the promised land of each new day. I am open to the miracles that the present holds out as its gift to me in the eternal now.

I surrender my focus on the past that I might dwell fully in the present. May my mind not wander into the darkness of before, but rather be filled with the light of now. May my heart be open to the knowing that anything is possible in any moment, and God Himself is not held back by the fears or mistakes of yesterday. I forgive what has been, and embrace what is. I am at peace in the holiness of this instant, and release all else.

DAY 15

On the Miracle of the Present

It's nothing more than a mental habit to idealize another time, another condition, another reality. It is simply a way to avoid the reality of our lives right now. And in avoiding the reality of our present circumstances, we avoid the miracles they offer. Everyone does this because that's the way the ego mind works. But we can stare down this self-defeating habit and cultivate a truer perspective: that wherever we are is the perfect place, and whatever time it is now is the perfect time. That doesn't mean we can't or shouldn't improve things, particularly ourselves. But indulging the thought that if only we were somewhere else things would be better is a surefire way to experience pain.

Today I accept myself as I am.

Who God created is divinely perfect, and that includes me. I have made mistakes for which I atone, but my mistakes are not who I am. Today may I be who I am called to be, that my thoughts and actions might glorify love.

Within my heart, as within all hearts, there is the light of a divine creator. Nothing I have done, or that others have done; nothing I have thought, or that others have thought, can dim the light that dwells in me. I pray to see the perfection in others, that I might see it in myself. I pray for the strength to forgive all others, that I might forgive myself. I pray for the power to love all others, that I might love myself.

Today I will not be tempted by a false humility that would proclaim I am not enough. Indeed I am enough, as is everyone. May neither my wounded places, nor my weaknesses, nor my mistakes of the past obscure the light that dwells within me. Rather, may I accept myself with the tender mercies that God Himself has shown me. He creates anew in every moment the chance for me to shine. Through Him, for Him, and because of Him, I can.

No matter what the problem, the solution is love.

There is but one problem and one solution. All problems are a deviation from love, and all solutions are a return to it.

Whatever problems I face today, I will look for answers inside myself. I will search my heart for any lack of love . . . lack of forgiveness . . . lack of acceptance of my brother or myself. I will be lifted then to an illumined place, where wisdom and truth shall guide me. There I will find the answers that I seek.

Dear God,

May I not be tempted today
To put blame on others.
I myself am the source of my healing,
as I allow You to change my mind.
May Your spirit guide me to a better place,
That my problems may disappear.

Amen.

The only path I am asked to monitor is my own.

I resist all temptation today to judge how I think others should behave. I cannot know the deeper forces at work within anyone's heart. My deliverance comes from accepting all people, not judging or controlling them.

I pray that when I am tempted to speak or act without charity, that God's spirit will correct my thoughts. I pray to be an instrument of love by which people are reminded of their innocence, not an instrument of blame that reminds them of their guilt. I do this for my own sake, that I too might be released from feelings of guilt that would otherwise bind me.

It is not my job to monitor anyone's journey, to know what's right or wrong for others, or to try to control their behavior. My salvation lies in deep acceptance of people exactly as they are, that I might know the inner peace that such acceptance brings. Amen.

My true self is a being of light and love. Today may I be my true self.

Today I remember who I really am. I am a child of God, created changeless and divinely perfect. While I have made mistakes and might surely make more, I accept that the spirit within me remains innocent and pure. I forgive others their trespasses that I might feel forgiven for my own, for all of us are light and all of us are love.

Today I resist the temptation to punish or undermine myself. All mistakes are a betrayal of self, and today I honor the goodness of my being. I resist any worldly projection onto me that I am less than the perfect child of God. Thus I am able to celebrate and truly enjoy my life.

Today I see past the filter of my shame and guilt, to the acceptance that nothing I have ever done or could ever do can diminish the light of my true being. God created me eternally innocent, and within my spirit so I remain. Having atoned for my errors, I am free to remember that God's spirit is alive in me.

DAY 20

On the Promise of the Present

The eternal self dwells in eternity, and eternity intersects linear time at only one point: the present. Who you are in this moment, therefore, is who you truly are. And who you are is love itself. From that essential point of perfect being, created anew by God in every instant, miracles flow naturally. Love interrupts the past and opens the future to new probabilities. No matter who you are, no matter how young or old you are, in the present, all things are possible.

Negativity poisons my mind, and positivity restores it.

I have a choice whether to join in the darkness of the world, its petty judgments, and constant blame. When I do so I inject my psyche with poison, and today I choose a healthy mind.

I replace all negativity with a positive attitude, in which I seek to find, and to articulate, the good in every heart. If I disagree, I will disagree with honor. If I debate a point, I will debate with respect. If I need to draw a line for the sake of justice, I will do so with an honor for the dignity of all.

I will no longer be careless with the working of my mind. Rather, I will use it as it was created by God to be used, as a conduit for love and a gateway to peace. May everyone, including myself, feel the tenderness of my approval and not the harshness of my unkindness.

I dedicate my work today to the furtherance of all things good.

Whether I am paid or not, whether I am working out in the world or planting my own garden, I dedicate whatever I am doing today to the uplifting of all things. May the activity of my mind and work of my hands be of service to the healing of the world.

Today I remember that there is only one work: to be who I am capable of being, to do what I am capable of doing to make the world a better place. May my life be of use to something greater than myself, that I might feel the joy of being used.

Dear God,

Today I dedicate all I am and all that I have,
That love might use me as a conduit of its power.
Illumine my mind and increase my understanding,
Hone my personality and deepen my skills,
That all I do might glorify Your presence in the world.
And so it is.

Amen.

Today I recognize the miracle in all things.

How often do I not notice the miracles all around me, or honor all the kindnesses shown me, or allow myself to fully embrace the good that's in my life? Today I remember that every day is precious, every heart carries within it the spirit of God, and every event contains the platform for a miracle. May I not be blind today to the awesomeness of life.

May the days be gone when I took for granted all the blessings in my life. May my eyes be open, that I might see more beauty; may my ears be open, that I might hear more truth; may my spirit open, that I might feel the tender touch of God.

Today I see through a different set of eyes, that I will recognize the miracles all around. I see the sparkle of light that surrounds all things and the yearning for love that exists in everyone. I see the innocence beyond all guilt and the love beyond all fear. And thus I am reborn into the truth of who I am.

I dwell in peace, knowing that God is here and God is good.

Sometimes I search for God, though God is in my mind. Sometimes I wait for truth, when truth is in my heart. And sometimes I allow the appearances of the world to obscure God's goodness.

But not today. Today I know I need to do nothing and I need to go nowhere, to experience God's love. For wherever I am, closer than my breath is God Himself with His arms around me. I am safe and secure in knowing this. I am blessed by what I know.

May I not be tempted by the darkness of the world to think that God is gone, or lured into the thinking of the world to ever doubt love's power. God is here, love is real, and I am safe. These things I know and will not forget. And so it is. Amen.

REFLECTION

On Saying Yes to
New Beginnings

Our very cells respond to the thoughts we think. With every word, silent or spoken, we participate in the body's functioning. We participate in the functioning of the universe itself. If our consciousness grows lighter, then so does everything within and around us. This means, of course, that with every thought, we can start to re-create our lives. In saying yes to new beginnings, we begin to bring them forth.

I greet all whom I meet today
with the love of God.

It can be a kind smile, an understanding pause, a touch of a hand that makes all the difference in how someone's day unfolds. I wish to be a conduit of love to those I meet, that I might know a softer way of being and a deeper sense of peace.

Let me remember today that all of us are in need of love, both those who make it obvious and those who make it easy to forget. Whether showing their love or hiding it, my brothers are, as I am, in need of understanding. May I be someone who understands.

May my selfish nature melt away, dear God, and compassion come to take its place. May everyone I meet or even think of today be blessed by the love I send their way. I will receive as I decide to give, and today I choose to give love.

The universe intends that I be loved. All is planned for my greater good.

As the handwriting of God, the universe both self-organizes and self-corrects. Through love I am connected to a pattern of perfection. All problems in the world—from the subtle to the immense—derive from someone having lost connection to the love within their hearts.

Today I plant myself within love's universe, that I may dwell within the miraculous matrix. As I align my thoughts and actions with love, I experience my greater good. I trust the universe to create through me ever-increasing dimensions of peace and joy.

I do not know how to control the universe, nor do I need to. The universe is controlled by love and love alone. Outside love's embrace the world is chaos, but within it all is safe and secure. Today I choose the arms of love in which to rest my soul.

My soul is imprinted with the yearning to be more.

Just as a flower bends toward the sun, I bend toward the lure of spirit. In my heart I am restless, for I know I am called to the greatness of my true being. Let me not tarry in my weaker places.

I am given otherworldly help today as I reach for what is possible. Angels herald my birth into the glory of who I really am. A mere nod in their direction, the slightest invitation for spirit to enter, and my mind becomes a touchstone for the thoughts that take me there.

I pray for guidance and strength today, to become the person I long to be and do the things I long to do. I honor the imprint of God upon my soul, and the yearning of my heart to follow the path He lays before me.

I am never abandoned, and never lost. I am held in the arms of God.

At times it feels I am alone in a dangerous world. I am hurt by life and cannot feel the embrace of a loving God. Yet such times as these cry out for faith. A sun that is eclipsed is not a sun forever hidden.

God never turns his face from me, nor rejects my prayers. His spirit resides within my mind, to guide my thoughts to the thoughts of peace. I am never left without His comfort. I am not separate from the source of my creation.

May my Internal Teacher remind me always that I am one with God. I am not separate or apart from love. I bend my thoughts in the direction of love for myself and others, that I might be delivered from the pain of a fearful world. Amen.

REFLECTION

On Life as a Spiral

According to ancient Asian philosophy, life is not a circle but a spiral. Every life lesson that has ever been presented to you (which means everything you have ever been through) will come back again, in some form, until you learn it. And the stakes each time will be higher. Whatever you've learned will bear greater fruit. Whatever you've failed to learn will bear harsher consequences. Whatever didn't work in your life before this point was a reflection of the fact that you hadn't yet integrated the different parts of yourself. Where you didn't yet accept yourself, you attracted a lack of acceptance in others. Where you hadn't yet dealt with your shadows, you manifested shadowy situations. Broken parts of you encountered broken parts of others. So now you know! That was then and this is now.

What you suffered through, you learned from. What you atoned for, became a path to self-improvement. All that you have lived through has taught you what it means to live at all.

With every breath,
I breathe in God's love.

E ndless love and power are available to me, whenever I re-member who I am. I am a child of the universe, a thought in the Mind of God, forever surrounded and sustained by the substance of divine mind.

I open my mind today to the remembrance of my true nature and the nature of the universe. I open my mind and I open my eyes today to the love that is all around me. With every breath, I drink in the holy substance that infuses all things.

On this day I remember and will not forget that love is all around me. I acknowledge love's presence in myself and others, and breathe in with every breath all the power it bestows.

My body's cells are suffused with light.

My body is a gift, enabling me to ground my spiritual journey within the illusion of time and space. It is neither my ultimate reality nor my true identity. I use the body as it was meant to be used—as a vessel through which to express my love.

I protect my body from the assaults of modernity—from the thoughts of fear to the contaminants of the physical environment. I do so by infusing my body with the light of the divine, seeing with my inner eye the spirit of God as it pours into every cell.

Dear God,

I dedicate to you my body.
Pour into it Your spirit.
Protect it from the forces of fear
And use it for Your purposes.
Turn my body into a holy thing.
And so it is.

Amen.

I forgive myself,
as God would have me do.

What God created is eternal, and what God made perfect shall remain so forever. Our mistakes do not uncreate the love in which we were created. Though I have made mistakes, I atone for them and accept God's release from any continuing consequences. His mercy is built into the structure of the universe.

I feel God's mercy as I extend mercy to others. Today I walk a softer way, holding neither myself nor others to the cross of my condemnation.

I will not use my mind today to attack whom God loves. I atone for errors that I have made, I seek to make amends and to be today who I was not before. May my actions now align with God's love within me. I forgive myself, as I know He forgives me, for the mistakes that I have made.

I surrender my mind to God.

While my mind can go in a million directions, I pray today that it go toward love. May wildness in my mind and heart no longer foster chaos. May the peace of God within me bring all chaos to an end.

Seeking order in my universe, I eschew at last the intemperate mind. I place my mind in the hands of God. I pray to be released from fear, that I might know true love.

Dear God,

Please stop the storms within me.
Make peaceful my mind and calm my heart.
Reveal to me the love around me,
That my fear might fall away.

Amen.

DAY 35

REFLECTION

On Re-Enchanting the World

We were all indoctrinated into a disenchanted world, and we've sacrificed a lot in order to live there. The world isn't better off for having forfeited its tenderness. The meanness and cynicism of our age, the reflexive sarcasm that passes for intelligent reflection, the suspicion and judgment of everyone and everything—such are the toxic by-products of a disenchanted worldview. Many of us want off that wheel of suffering. We don't want to accept that what is is what has to be. We want to pierce the veil of illusion that separates us from a world of infinite possibility. We want another kind of life—for ourselves and for the world. We are considering that there might be another way—a door to miraculous realms that is simply waiting to be opened.

Whatever I give to others, I am giving to myself.

In the mortal world, what I give away is no longer mine. In the spiritual world, only what I give away is mine. If I give anger, I shall know anger. If I give love, then I shall know love.

Help me resist, dear God, my projection of blame onto others. For it is only in seeing them innocent that I can be at peace. Help me to disagree without blame, to share without criticism, and to debate without demonizing anyone. Make me in all ways a conduit of your love.

Today I give my peace to others, that I might be at peace. I withhold my judgment, that I not be judged. I extend my love, that love be forever mine.

Today I rest within the softness of my heart.

The ego mind would lead me astray, to arrogant attitudes and puffed-up airs. In fact it is my spirit self, my humble self, that makes me shine and calls forth my good.

In my humble place I am strong, for the power of God can then move through me. While arrogance hides my beauty, humility makes it visible. In my humility, I step back and let God's miracle work through me.

Today I rest within the softness of my heart, and in that place I am lifted up. The universe registers the power within me, as I give all power to God.

May my mind be a touchstone for love today.

M ay I be divinely programmed today to think thoughts that are the most creative, positive, insightful, and beneficial. In doing so, I do not give up personal responsibility or turn my power over to something outside myself; rather, I take the highest level of responsibility, asking God to make my mind a literal touchstone for His love.

As I think with love, I co-create with God a space for miraculous breakthroughs. I walk forward in confidence today, having prayed that my mind will be used for holy purposes.

I pray that God's spirit overshadow my mind today, rearranging all false perceptions and uplifting them to divine right order. May wrong-minded perceptions dissolve in the presence of endless love for myself and others. Amen.

Enlightenment
is my goal today.

The journey of enlightenment is a journey of the mind: from a focus on the body to a focus on spirit, from a limited sense of self to an unlimited sense of self, from a sense of separateness to a sense of unity with all things, from blame to blessing, and from fear to love.

This journey of my mind and heart—not always easy but always miraculous—changes every aspect of my life. It transforms my nervous system, my energy, and my internal state of being. It leads to changes in my behavior and to shifts in how others respond to me.

As enlightenment becomes my goal, my life is free to transform. I release my attachment to lower things, allowing my mind to be guided into higher realms. Fear dissolves, and my love flows forth. I am redeemed and I am changed.

REFLECTION

On Awakening

I f you want to believe that what your physical eyes can see is all that's there, then fine, you can. Stay in that small fraction of perceptual reality if you choose. But at some point, even if that point is at the point of death, we all know better. I've seen cynics become mystics on their deathbeds. We are here as though in a material dream, from which the spiritual nature of our larger reality is calling us to awaken. The magician, the alchemist, the miracle-worker, is simply someone who has woken up to the material delusions of the world and decided to live another way. In a world gone mad, we can choose to be sane. In order to move ourselves, and our civilization, into the next phase of our evolutionary journey, it's time for all of us to awaken.

The spiritual path
is my only path.

Today I remember that every event is a part of my spiritual journey. Every moment is a moment on my spiritual path, inviting me to rise to the highest version of myself.

May grace, compassion, understanding, and love be the hallmarks of my personality, as they are the essence of my true being. May heaven come to earth through me today.

Dear God,

I am willing today
To be the person you would have me be.
I release to you my illusions.
Please strengthen me where I am weak
And heal me where I am wounded.
And so it is.

Amen.

May who I am today be
a positive influence on the
lives of those around me.

Every thought we think, every word we say, every action
we take has an effect on the universe. Other people feel
what we're thinking, whether they're conscious of this or not.

Surrendering our lives to God is the ultimate taking of personal responsibility, as God is not outside but within us. In
surrendering our lives to him, we pray that his love move into
and through us, as a light unto the world.

Dear God,

Today may I be a conduit for Your love.
May Your peace, through me, bring peace to all the world.

Amen.

Let me be guided by the wisdom of my heart.

Our physical eyes don't register the deepest truth of who we are, what's truly happening, or what things mean. There is, however, an inner eye, the opening of which is the purpose of our lives.

Today I will extend my perception beyond what my physical eyes can see. Saluting the love that lies beyond a veil of physical appearances, I will invoke a world that lies beyond. My eyes will open to a truer truth.

I will not be blinded by the world today. I will not be guided by worldly sight alone. I seek true vision, that I might see. Amen.

Today I bear witness to the agony of the world, praying to be used as a healing force.

Let me not forget today the needless suffering of so many. I do not dwell on this suffering, but I bear witness with a compassionate heart.

May I not be tempted today to attend to my own pain while minimizing the suffering of others. May I not be swayed today by the insidiousness of selfishness. Placing myself in service to the healing of the world, I gain greater perspective and a more powerful consciousness.

Dear God,

Today I remember those whom the world has forgotten:
Those who are tortured,
Those who are oppressed,
Those who are hopeless and feel no love around them.
May the love I send to them
Help work miracles in their lives.

Amen.

REFLECTION

On Our True Father/Mother

We can help release the drama of our childhood by re-defining whose child we are. We are products of our family of origin, to be sure. But who is that, exactly—our mortal parentage, or our immortal one? It's an important distinction, because we inherit the legacy of whomever we think sourced us. We might have inherited limitation and fear from our mortal parents, but we inherited miracles and love from God. Our worldly parents might have been wonderful people or they might have been scoundrels, but the larger point is that they're not who created us. Superman was only *raised* by those nice people in Kansas. Understanding that God is our true Father/Mother, and all humanity our brothers and sisters, delivers us to a more respectful attitude toward our biological family, and more able to receive the inheritance of God.

I give my life to God today.

Today I will not burden myself by thinking I need to run the universe. I needn't control anyone or anything. I need only to show up fully with my heart and in my excellence.

I surrender everything to God, who lives within me. Every burden and decision I place in His hands. I know that as I do so I will be led to divine right thought and action. The universe will arrange itself on my behalf.

How wonderful it is to relax at last and fall back into the arms of God. It is not a stiff neck but a soft heart that will guide my course of action. I will not forget to trust in God today.

I will not be falsely humble today.

The thinking of the world is upside down, and one of the ways in which our thoughts are inverted is in the area of arrogance and humility. It isn't arrogant, but humble, for me to accept that the power of God is within me. What is arrogant is to think otherwise.

Many of my problems have arisen because I chose to play small, denying the power of my mind, the power of my love, my own power to work miracles. I was born with spiritual wings, and I am meant to spread them. Today I will not be falsely humble, but will own in all ways the power of my love and forgiveness to work miracles in my life.

Today I recognize that while my power is neither more nor less than anyone else's, it is the power of God within me. Through the power of my love, I pave the way today out of darkness and into light for both myself and those around me. Amen.

I needn't prove anything to anyone. I am blessed as a child of God.

I needn't compensate for any lack in myself, for there is no lack in a child of God. I am whole and complete as a spiritual being; I need do nothing to augment what is already perfect.

In any moment when I puff myself up, I appear less radiant. In any moment when I am defenseless and humble, I am radiant with God's love and power. Today I will be defenseless and safe in the arms of God.

Dear God,

Please remove any armor in front of my heart,
And all barriers to my love.
Take away my insecurities,
And remind me of my intrinsic value.
Let me not be tempted to inflate who I am,
Which will only diminish me and decrease my joy.

Amen.

I meet limited circumstances with unlimited thoughts.

While the world is changeable, the Truth is not. May I not be tempted by the drama of the world to forget the eternal peace of God. May I hold to the truth of who I really am and how the universe operates, despite whatever the world may say.

In a universe where only love is real, I need not be deterred by the appearances of fear. Where there is lack in the material world, I proclaim the infinite abundance of the spiritual universe. Where there is discord and conflict on the material plane, I proclaim the love that unites us as one.

Today I meet limits with the thinking of unlimited possibility. Whatever occurs, I remember that miracles are possible regardless of circumstance. I proclaim the miracle, I pray for the miracle, and I rejoice in the miracle. Amen.

REFLECTION

On Your Preferred Life

Take a good look at your life right now. If you don't like something about it, close your eyes and imagine the life you want. Now allow yourself to focus your inner eye on the person you would have to be in order to create your preferred life. Notice the differences in how you behave and present yourself; allow yourself to spend several seconds breathing in the new image, expanding your energy into this new mold. Hold the image for several seconds and ask God to imprint it on your subconscious mind. Do that every day for ten minutes or so. If you share this technique with certain people, the chances are good they'll tell you that it's way too simple. It's up to you what you choose to believe.

Dear God,

Please impress upon me
The vision of whom I am meant to be.
Reveal to me the bigger life
That You would have me live.
Undo the forces that keep me bound,
That I might serve You more.

Amen.

In God all things are possible.

There is no order of difficulty in miracles. One is not harder than another. With God, all things are possible. And I am one with God.

We can only have what we allow ourselves to have. I will not close my eyes today and then bemoan the darkness. I will not miss out on miracles by denying they exist. I am open to receive the blessings that faith in love bestow.

May I not constrict my mind today. I am open to the possibility of infinite possibility. I am open to the unlimited good that the universe has in store for me. I know that in God there are endless miracles, and they are meant for me.

Time and space are servants, not the masters of who I am.

I am a being of spirit, not merely flesh. Spirit is not a servant, but master of the material world. As I remember who I really am, I place myself under the laws of the spiritual universe.

In the spiritual universe, there is only abundance, only good, only peace, and only love. By remembering spirit is my true identity as well as my true home, I raise myself above the limits of the mortal world.

I am held back by nothing today. Seeing beyond the three-dimensional plane, I invoke the world beyond it. There is nothing my holiness cannot do. Neither time nor space are more powerful than God, for He alone is the King of the universe.

I see no one as guilty today.

It is my choice whether to focus on someone's guilt or innocence. It is my choice whether to blame or bless. It is my choice whether to limit my perception to someone's body, or to release myself to the knowledge of the innocence that lies in everyone.

Which choice I make determines my experience of myself, and thus my world. If I see guilt in others, I will feel guilty. If I release my attachment to the guilt in others, I will feel released myself.

God does not need me to police His universe. He needs me only to forgive.

Dear God,

Please remove from my mind
Any tendency to judge
Whom I know you love.
For I know you love us all.

Amen.

There is no limit to my potential, for I am unlimited in God.

In each of us there lies unlimited potential, no more or less in me than in anyone. Today I accept with humility and grace the fact that this is so.

God is great, and God is alive in me. I open myself to receive His spirit, His wisdom, and His power today. May I not be limited by any thought that I am less than He created me to be.

I strive today to be a living embodiment of God's love. However I might fail at times, I know His spirit will always guide me back to the truth that lives within me. May every step I take be a step toward love.

REFLECTION

On Embracing What's Important

We spend so much time on unimportant things—things with no ultimate meaning—yet for reasons no one seems to fully understand, such nonessentials stand at the center of our worldly existence. They have no connection to our souls whatsoever, yet they have attached themselves to our material functioning. Like spiritual parasites, these things eat away our life force and deny us our joy. The only way to rid ourselves of their pernicious effects is to walk away . . . not from things that need to get done, but from thoughts that need to die.

Crossing the bridge to a better world begins with crossing a bridge inside our minds, from the addictive mental patterns of fear and separation, to enlightened perceptions of unity and love. We're in the habit of thinking fearfully, and it takes spiritual discipline to turn that around in a world where love is more suspect than fear. To achieve a miraculous experience of life, we must embrace a more spiritual perspective. Otherwise, we will leave this earth one day without ever having known the real joy of living.

In realizing who I really am, I unleash my power as a child of God.

It is not what I do, but who I am, that generates my power on the earth. For my power does not come from a worldly source; my power comes from God.

As I relax each day into the knowledge of my spiritual source, my true identity is revealed to me. I align myself with the truth of my being, my home in God, and from that place all good emerges. Every thought, every feeling, every action becomes infused with the light and glory of God.

I rest in the knowledge that I need to do nothing to increase my intrinsic value. I am in God, as God is in me. I find stillness and power in the realization that this is so.

In choosing love,
I cast out fear.

I will see today what I choose to see. If I choose to see guilt, then it will be there; but then I will not see innocence. If I choose to see innocence, it will be there; and then I will not see guilt.

Perception is my choice, and I do not pretend today that I am powerless before my decision. I accept that every perception is a choice, and today I choose to see love. I will discern, but I will not judge.

May my mind be disciplined today, to see past guilt to the love that lies beyond it. In myself and in everyone, may I see the innocent and pure and true. Love is my power to invoke the manifestation of what I choose to see.

⚘ May I see all the beauty
around me today.

Often I'm so lost in my illusions that I do not see the beauty of the world, or hear the music of the world, or feel the love in the world. Today I choose to be aware of them all.

How often I hide away from the gorgeous manifestations around me. From the beauties of nature to the tenderness of friendship, the miracles of the world often fade from my view without my really having seen them. Today may this not be so.

Today I see all the evidence that the world is a wonderful place. May I not fall asleep to the miracles around me. I embrace what the world has to give to me, and I give thanks that it is so.

May God use me today.

Love will save the world, but only if we express it. May everything I do today be an expression of God's love.

May I be a channel for love today, co-creating with God a more perfect world. With every thought of love, I create a miracle. Every time I withhold love, I deflect one. Today may I only love.

Dear God,

Use my hands and feet,
My words and actions today.
Use who I am and what I do
To help You heal the world.

Amen.

REFLECTION

On Giving Birth to Our Spiritual Selves

It isn't easy, giving birth to our spiritual potential. Spiritual labor can be very arduous—one holy instant at a time, when we give up, surrender, soften, don't care if we're right, forgo our impatience, detach from the opinions and prizes of the world, and rest in the arms of God. But the end result is the love of our lives. We begin to feel more comfortable within ourselves, less laden by the chronic angst that marks the times in which we live. We begin to feel free at last of past hurts, able to fearlessly love again. We begin to exhibit the maturity and strength that were lacking in our personalities before. A new energy emanates from who we are, and others can see it too.

Today I make a stand for love.

It is important that I stand my ground today. I stand for wisdom. I stand for integrity. I stand for honesty. I stand for compassion. I stand for clarity. I stand for forgiveness. I stand for love.

May these not be merely words today, but rather the field of my experience. May I gather up my internal forces and lead the life I was created to live.

May I not be lukewarm today, but rather deeply committed to the principles I believe in. Who am I to be lazy when I have been called by God to greatness. May I not forget today the importance of the ground on which I stand.

May I have the strength to forgive those who've betrayed me.

Not everyone has shown me kindness or mercy, but still I have a choice. May I not remain attached to past betrayals, but rather allow forgiveness to set me free.

What I forgive, I am not condoning. I am merely placing in the hands of God what is not mine to fix. I bless those who have betrayed me, for only in seeing their innocence can I see mine.

Dear God,

I am willing to see beyond the guilt
That hides my brother's light from me.
I need Your help to do this, though,
For my pain has been very great.

Amen.

DAY 63

I want a bigger heart today.

May I not be guided by a narrow mind, nor hindered by a miserly heart. May I not be limited by false beliefs, or swayed by pernicious thoughts.

Today I want a bigger heart, that I might have a freer soul. May all who meet or even think of me be aware that they are loved.

Dear God,

Expand my heart today.
Enlighten my mind and increase my love
That I might be like You.

Amen.

Love is always pregnant
with the next best thing.

Life is always brewing more of itself. The universe is infinitely creative and never stops arranging opportunities to love.

No matter what happened even a moment before, the present is always a new beginning. God's Mind rearranges time and space according to our willingness to love. Nothing in the world can stop the creative power of the universe.

Let me not forget that the universe is endlessly creating opportunities, following my lead whenever I choose to love. As I open my heart, life will birth itself through me. I will be amazed to see what comes forth from my heart. Amen.

REFLECTION

On the Alchemy of Personal Transformation

It's when we face the darkness squarely in the eye—in ourselves and in the world—that we begin at last to see the light. And that is the alchemy of personal transformation. In the midst of the deepest, darkest night, when we feel most humbled by life, the faint shadow of our wings begins to appear. Only when we have faced the limits of what we can do, does the limitlessness of what God can do begin to dawn on us. It is the depth of the darkness now confronting our world that will reveal to us the magic of who we truly are. We are spirit, and thus we are more than the world. When we remember that, the world itself will bow to our remembrance.

Let others think with mercy toward me, and may I think with mercy toward them.

How often I'm reminded of God's mercy toward me, as over and over I have made mistakes and been allowed to begin again. Surely God's mercy is woven into the nature of the universe.

May I show mercy to others as God has shown mercy toward me. May I not withhold my gracious allowance for the mistakes of the mortal self. Rather, may others feel from me the charity and compassion of one who understands.

Dear God,

May I not withhold from others
The mercy You have shown to me.
May I not remind others of their mistakes,
But rather be a space
Where people feel free to begin again.

Amen.

Today I will be a friend to myself.

No one is going to accept me if I don't accept myself first. When anyone has rejected me, I realize now that I had rejected myself first. I was waiting for someone else's acceptance to prove to me that I was worth accepting! Not accepting myself, I didn't show up in the fullness of myself when I engaged with others. And so of course they rejected me!

Today I will be loyal to myself. Not in denial about my weaknesses, but loyal . . . and kind . . . and embracing. I will accept myself warts and all. Other people will see my goodness when I have seen it first.

No one knows better than I do all the hell that I have been through. I will no longer beat up on myself, when I know so well the blows I have endured. Starting today, I will be a better friend to myself.

I am never forgotten by God.

Something is always happening under the surface of things. Pieces rearrange themselves. Love reveals itself. Life reasserts itself.

I am part of the universe; I am woven into the fabric of divine existence. There is a natural pull toward ever-increasing good that is built into my soul. I am never forgotten by God.

Dear God,

You are always guiding my life
In the direction of my higher good.
Help me to remember that I am one with You
And never separate.
Help me to surrender,
That I might know my greater joy.

Amen.

I will walk
my own path today.

I may or may not be liked by everyone. Not everyone will see things as I do, or feel what I feel, or think what I think. Only my belief that they should can cause me pain.

I will seek to live my authentic truth, regardless of whether it is a solitary path. I will not try to "fit in" to the crowd today, but rather I will seek to discern more clearly the path that is mine to walk.

Dear God,

Help me find Your will for me,
That I may not be tempted by the will of the world.
May Yours be the only voice I hear.
May I see the path You would have me walk,
And may I walk it without fear.

Amen.

REFLECTION

On Recognizing Our Source

According to *A Course in Miracles,* what we have is an "authorship" problem. Not recognizing our divine source, we express ourselves as creations of the world rather than as creations of spirit. The world has imprinted upon our psyches its brokenness and pain. And there is no point in trying to heal that pain until we heal our misplaced sense of heritage. We are not children of the world; we are children of God. We don't have to allow the false input of a weary world to affect us as it does.

Confusion about our divine heritage translates into confusion about ourselves: not understanding who we are or where we come from, we find it hard to understand who we are now or where we are now. And so we lack spiritual stability. In the absence of the sense of a divine creator, the mind assumes that we're our own creator and thus our own God. If God isn't the big cheese, then *I* must be the big cheese! And that thought—that we're it, we're the greatest—is not merely narcissism. It's a psychosis that permeates the human condition.

In remembering the truth of where we came from, we become more open to the truth of who we are.

I place my mind
in service to love.

When I think without love, I am not thinking at all. Unloving thoughts but make illusions. I wish to be awake today to truer truths, the love beyond our mortal fears.

I proactively make the choice today to place my mind in service to love, so I can experience the miracles only love can bring. May I not be tempted to forget my function as a bringer of love to everyone.

Dear God,

Please send Your spirit to illuminate my mind.
May all my thoughts lead me into love
And away from fear.
May love light my way all day.

Amen.

Today I claim
the power of love.

Let me cleave to love in moments when I am tempted by fear. May I remember that there is nothing love cannot do. There is no feeling, circumstance, situation, or relationship so filled with fear that love cannot transform it. Today I claim the power of love.

May my mind be so aligned with love that its power within me feels natural. I wield the power to work miracles with humility and grace.

There is no situation my love will not transform, if I look at everyone through the eyes of forgiveness. I claim the power that love brings with it, to deliver my world from fear to love. Today I do not just believe in love; I claim its power as my own.

My greatest power is the power to change my mind.

No matter what is happening, no one but me can determine what I choose to think. I can choose to believe in miracles. I can choose to have faith in the goodness of others regardless of how they express themselves.

By doing so, I develop the power of my spiritual mind. I develop the power to invoke the world I wish to see. When I believe in people's goodness, they are more likely to show me their goodness. When I believe in the possibility of miracles, I'm more likely to experience them. I will not be deterred today by the spiritual ignorance of the worldly mind.

May I see beyond the veil today, that I might invoke the miraculous. May I see beyond the probable, to what I know in my heart is possible. Today I will exercise the power of the spiritual mind.

I am not afraid to show love today.

Sometimes I am afraid that if I show my love, my vulnerability, my fear, then I will be in danger. What a sad misunderstanding that is. For only when I show my love can I be truly seen.

Only in letting down my guard can I appear to others in the light of my true self. Only in my softness does my tenderness reveal itself. Only in my defenselessness does my true safety lie. I pray to be a gentler version of myself

Dear God,

Remove the walls I have constructed around my heart.
Remove the barriers that obstruct my love,
That I might give and receive it.
Remove my fears, that I might dwell in peace
And share my peace with everyone.

Amen.

REFLECTION

On Aging

If we don't exercise our bodies, then our muscles begin to constrict. And if we don't exercise our minds, then our attitudes begin to constrict. Nothing constricts our life experiences like the constriction of our thoughts. It limits our possibilities, and it limits our joy. We have all seen people who've aged with sorrow; we've seen others as well who've aged with joy. It's time to intend to age with joy, deciding that the joy of youth is a good kind of joy, but it's not the only kind. In fact, there is a joy in knowing that after all these years, we've finally grown up. We've finally come to know ourselves. We're finally at home in our own skin.

I send my love
to everyone today.

As I enter any situation, may my love be sent before me. Any room I enter, I blast with all my love.

Thus will my life be blessed, and the forces of chaos remain at bay. I throw light upon all things, that darkness cannot dwell there. I proactively call forth the love that then casts out all fear.

I dedicate my mind to the miraculous, to the world beyond this one and to the joy that is available there. May every thought I think help penetrate the veil that hides the light from everyone. My love is a mighty force for good.

I choose to dwell in the universe of love.

I may encounter many reasons to get upset today, to be angry, to judge or blame others or myself. I can dwell within that universe, or I can choose again.

There is another world, a truer world, where only peace exists. No one is blamed or judged or attacked, but rather love is used to heal all things. I need not dwell in the universe of darkness; I can choose to dwell in the universe of love.

May my mind not wander into dark terrain today, but may I remain within the field of light. May I not be tempted to attack my brother, or attack myself. May I cleave instead to love.

I see beyond guilt to innocence today.

Forgiveness is "selective remembering"—a conscious decision to focus on love and let the rest go. The ego is relentless, and it will subtly and insidiously try to convince me of my brother's guilt. I will not listen to the voice of my ego today.

May the spirit of God deliver me today from the temptation to judge, to find fault, to criticize. May I be saved from my tendency to condemn. May my eyes be opened to the innocence in everyone.

Only when I see the light in others, can I remember that it is in me. Only in extending the light to others, can I be at peace myself. Only through forgiveness can I be set free.

I place myself in service to the love that heals all things.

There is no one more deserving than I to wear the mantle of God's peace and power. There is no one more special, or less special, than me. For all of us are one.

Today I accept the mantle of God's love, to be drawn around my shoulders and assign to me His power. May others find in me a rest for their souls, as the love of God extends through me to bring all beings peace.

I accept with humility the peace of God, bestowed upon me, that I might be a conduit through which He bestows it on the world. I place myself in service to the love that heals all things, and pray to be used in the highest, best way.

REFLECTION

On the Holiness of a
Quiet Moment

There's a way of relaxing into our center, letting other people have their say, knowing our being is even more radiant at times when we're in a space of not-doing. When the ego steps back, the power of God steps forward. Too often we feel we're invisible unless we're making the cool comment, doing this or doing that. But we're so much more powerful when grounded in silence. Taking a deep breath, knowing that what we don't say can be as powerful as what we do say, thinking deeply about something before making a response— such actions leave room for the spirit to flow, to harmonize our circumstances and move them in a more positive direction. How many times have we felt we've blown it simply by talking when we later wish we hadn't, or by showing off when we could have just sat there and seemed intriguing?

God's spirit will always reveal the truth to us if we simply don't block His guidance. And we block it by talking first, attitudinally walking ahead of truth. This happens when we push too hard, trying frantically to make things happen, or keep things from happening, because we lack faith in an invisible order of things. That is why a holy instant matters: it is a moment of quiet when the spirit enters and makes right all things.

Only in my mind does 🕊 the past exist.

Only in my mind does the past exist. Today I atone for the errors of my past and forgive others for theirs as well. Thus I am free of the consequences of wrong-minded thought and action.

Today I dwell in the eternal present. In any moment I am free to restart my life. I am not held back by the mistakes of my past, as I atone for them in my heart. Freeing myself from the chains of the past, I free the future to be unlike it.

May the love in my heart today interrupt the patterns of the past. I release the future as I release the past, knowing love will make all things right. Dwelling fully in the present, I release both past and future to a higher place.

I free the universe from my efforts to control it.

I cannot control the universe, though I act at times as though I can. The universe is planned for divine right functioning, and my efforts to control it only interrupt God's plan.

Today I release the reins that are not mine to begin with. I will not try to control the world, on any level or in any way. I free all things and people from the shackles of my self-will.

How different my life will be if I let go, allowing the universe to do its dance without my constant interference. Today I release the thought that I know what is best—for myself, for the world, or for anyone in it. I relax into the patterns of a divinely orchestrated universe, asking only to be guided where I can best fit in and be used in service to love's will.

As long as I am in service, I am in the flow of divine love.

The organizing principle of all life is service. Every cell serves the functioning of the organism of which it is a part. The sun serves life by sharing its warmth and light. The rain serves the earth by pouring water on growing things. Plants serve life by giving us oxygen and food.

We, too, find our right place in the universe when we place ourselves in service to life. As long as I enter any situation with the primary goal of being of service, being of use to the furtherance of goodness and love, I will find my place and find my peace.

May all that I think and do be in service to a higher love. May my personal goals be subsumed in my desire to serve. May I not be tempted to believe service entails sacrifice. May I always remember that the one I truly serve is myself.

God is the light
upon my path.

There's always more to any situation than meets the eye. Every person carries within them the seed of God, and every aspect of time and space carries the potential for miraculous unfoldment. It is not what is happening on the outside, but how we view it from the inside, that determines our grace within any situation and the joy we can derive from it.

I can see through the eyes of the world, or I can see through the eyes of love. One produces darkness, while the other produces light. Today I make a choice for life and love.

May God's hands be upon my shoulders that I might feel His love. May God's light be upon my vision that I might see things as they truly are.

REFLECTION

On True Forgiveness

True forgiveness is not a lack of discernment or the product of fuzzy thinking. It is the conscious choice to remember the love we experienced, and to let go of anything else as the illusion it really was. This doesn't make us more vulnerable to manipulation or exploitation; in fact, it makes us less so. For the mind that forgives is a mind that is closer to its true nature. The fact that I forgive you doesn't mean you "won." It doesn't mean you got away with something. It simply means I'm free to go back to the light, reclaim my inner peace, and stay there.

I surrender my sadness for God to heal.

W hen sadness overwhelms me, I can't cast it out with my rational mind. I can't analyze depression and expect it to dissolve. There are times when I need a miracle to rise above my tears.

Today, or any day when I feel overcome with grief, I'll remember that God wipes away all tears and He will wipe away mine. This period of sadness is painful but it is temporary. This too shall pass. So have we been promised by God, and His promises are real.

Dear God,

Please take away the sadness in my heart.
Send Your spirit to rearrange my thoughts,
That my emotions might heal.
Make my life again a happy place.

Amen.

DAY 87

Let my heart be guided by mercy today.

Today I remember that all people make mistakes. Let me not be harsh but magnanimous. May I show mercy to others as God has shown mercy to me.

All of us live in fear at times. May I be kinder today than I have been before, that all those around me—those who rise as well as those who fall—might feel from me the love of a friend.

Those who have shown me mercy have been angels in my life, creating a space for me to rise when I have fallen down. May I be that to others, and pass along the mercy that has been shown at times to me. Amen.

Today I seek to love those whom I do not like.

Like everyone, I have my prejudices—my opinions about those who do not agree with my view of the world. Yet my incapacity to love them is my own contribution to the fears that plague the planet. Today I seek to love even those I cannot bring myself to like.

I devote my day to blessing those whom I do not like, knowing that if I knew them as God knows them, then I would love them as He does. I ask not that they change but that I might see them more clearly. May their innocence become obvious to me.

Dear God,

I am willing to see the love
In those whom I cannot bring myself to like.
I am willing to see the innocence in those I judge
And the beauty in those I condemn.
Please heal my mind of its own darkness.

Amen.

Today I claim
my oneness with God.

When not at peace, I am separate from my true self. When not feeling love, I am separate from God. Today I claim my oneness with God so that my suffering shall end.

May false and delusional fractals of my true self—angry, needy, controlling, or whatever—go back now to the nothingness from whence they came. For they are not me, and today I embrace the experience of my true self.

May angels surround me and always remind me of the truth of who I really am, and the innocence in everyone. May I not be tempted by the falsehoods of the world to forget that I am one with God.

REFLECTION

On Beginning Again

In any given moment, the universe is primed to give us new life, to begin again, to create new opportunities, to miraculously heal all things, to change darkness to light and fear to love. God's light shines eternally clear, untarnished by our illusions. Our job is to take a deep breath, slow down, surrender all thoughts of past or future, and let the spirit shine forth in our awareness. God is not daunted by our nightmares of guilt; He is ever awake to how beautiful we are. He made us that way, and so it is.

The ego is powerless before the power of love.

Despite my illusions and the shrieks of my ego, there lies a changeless, undisturbable peace within me. Within it lies the answer to all my questions and the end to all my fears.

Today, even at moments when I cannot find that peace, I empower myself by remembering that it exists. My faith will break through all my illusions like a tiny flower through a crack in cement. Illusions will fall and peace will prevail, in my life and in the world.

Dear God,

Despite whatever thoughts in my mind
Might hide Your light today,
Please show me what I need to see.
I believe in Your power,
And I believe in Your love.
Today may I experience
That which I believe.

Amen.

I surrender my attachment to lesser things.

I know I've made idols of many things, thinking this or that would bring me joy. Yet only the experience of who I really am, at home at last within myself, will bring to me the peace I seek.

I surrender my attachments to people and places, riches and prestige, which my ego tells me would give me value. I know my value is alone in God. May I not be tempted to forget today that the light within me is beyond all value. I will but to remember this.

Dear God,

Heal my mind
Of the false belief that I need anything more
Than to remember love.
May the toys of the world
Not tempt me to forget
The grandeur that is You.

Amen.

I am hugely powerful today, for the power of God is in me.

My power is not something that might reveal itself at a later date. My power in the world is a result of my decision to reveal it. I am powerful in whatever moment I choose to be, for God is in my mind.

The power of God is the power to heal. As I surrender my thoughts to love, God's power moves through me and I become a healer. I am lifted up as a leader as I make myself a follower of the light of God within.

May the power of God move through me today, and make of me a powerful representative of His love on earth. May my smaller self be washed away. May His illumination shine through my personality, and reveal itself through me.

I throw light around
my problems today.

I align my thinking with the Mind of God, by aligning myself with love. In God all things are possible, and my mind is part of God's. May I co-create with God today the miracles of love.

What appears like a problem is merely a place where a miracle awaits. I shower my love on all my problems, that God's power might move through me and solve them. I depend on miracles, for there is no limit to what the love of God can do.

Dear God,

I place in Your hands
Every problem I have,
And I know they will be solved.
Miracles occur naturally for you, dear God,
And I know they are meant for me.

Amen.

DAY 95

REFLECTION

On Faith

My heart beats, my lungs breathe, my ears hear, my hair grows. And I don't have to make them work—they just do. Planets revolve around the sun, seeds become flowers, embryos become babies, and with no help from me. Their movement is built into a natural system. I am an integral part of that system, too. I can let my life be directed by the same force that makes flowers grow—or I can do it myself.

To trust in the force that moves the universe is faith. Faith isn't blind, it's visionary. Faith is believing that the universe is on my side, and that the universe knows what it's doing. Faith is a psychological awareness of an unfolding force for good, constantly at work in all dimensions. My attempt to direct this force only interferes with it. My willingness to relax into it allows it to work on my behalf. Without faith, I'm frantically trying to control what it is not my business to control, and fix what it is not in my power to fix. What I'm trying to control is much better off without me, and what I'm trying to fix can't be fixed by me anyway. Without faith, I'm wasting time.

In the spiritual universe, all of us are one.

Beyond a world of separate bodies, there is a world of spiritual unity. In the truer realms, there is no place where one of us stops and the other begins.

May I see beyond the veil today, to a world of unity and truth. There are no walls that separate us, no conflicts that are even real. In truth, there is only the love that unites us and makes us one in God.

Dear God,

May I see beyond the walls that appear
To separate me from others.
May I extend my love
Beyond the illusions of guilt and error.
May nothing hide the truth of my unity with
  everyone and everything.

Amen.

I choose to see innocence,
not guilt, today.

The body's eyes can find guilt anywhere. Only the heart can always see innocence.

That which I choose to focus on in others, I fortify within myself. If I see someone as guilty, I will feel guiltier. If I see them as innocent, I will feel more innocent. In the words of *A Course in Miracles,* "An idea doesn't leave its source." Every time I see anyone, depending on how I choose to think of them, I am deciding what I will see in me.

May my fear be nullified as I realize the love that lies within all of us. May my ego be quieted by a choir of angels. Thus I attain my power to work miracles, and my own inner peace. Only in seeing the beauty in others can I see it within myself.

As I focus on love, my fear will recede.

I see in life what I choose to see, for projections precede per-ception. And as I focus on anything, all evidence to the contrary begins to recede from my awareness.

If I'm looking for the positive, I won't notice the negative. If I'm looking for the negative, I won't notice the positive. The vision of a world of love costs me the vision of a world of fear, and the vision of a world of fear costs me the vision of a world of love. Such is the law that rules perception.

Dear God,

May my perceptions be purified.
May my eyes see love so clearly
That fear recedes from my awareness.
May a vision of peace
Reveal the real world to me
And all else fall away.

Amen.

I can be whoever
I choose to be today.

Who and how I was yesterday has no inherent connection to who and how I choose to be today. My present is not caused by my past, unless I choose that it be so. For in any given moment, regardless of circumstances, I can choose again. I can choose strength instead of weakness, and love instead of fear. I can choose to bless instead of blame, and to lean into the future rather than dragging with me the past.

The limits of yesterday have no power over the unlimited possibilities of this moment, for in God all things are possible and in God all things are programmed to be perfect. I make myself available to this moment, allowing the spirit of God to illuminate my heart.

Dear God,

May this present moment be a holy one,
In which nothing but Your light
Shines into my mind
And extends through me.

Amen.

REFLECTION

On Making Decisions

Because spirit is the part of our mind that remains in conscious contact with God, we can safely place all decisions in His hands. The mortal ego dwells in linear time and does not know the future; spirit dwells in eternity and therefore *does*. He knows not only what will happen in the future, but also how every decision made will affect every living thing forever. Imagine an infinitely complex computer that could reliably analyze any situation and give a readout, to the nth detail, of what would happen if this, this, or that were to occur. We don't get to see the readout, of course, but we are given simple instructions on how best to behave in order to support the highest outcome for ourselves and others. The instructions might come in a form as simple as an intuitive flash, or a complex process of growth and understanding that gradually unfolds within us. No matter what I need to decide, may God make the decision for me.

My true self is
a magnet for good.

My ego tells me I can make right my life, but only if I work hard enough. I grasp, I scramble, yet ultimately I meet failure and loss.

The spirit within is my salvation, like a magnet that draws all things into divine right order. God alone is the light with which I can see, the insight that gives me clarity, and the energy that lifts me above my fear. God is the power through which I rise.

I let go my efforts at trying to fix my world. Rather,
I seek peace in God. My outer kingdom will fall
into place once my inner one is filled with light.
May I be filled with You, dear God.
And may I only be filled with You.

Amen.

My vulnerability makes
me invulnerable.

Defenses, emotional walls, and rigidity do not serve to protect me. Rather, they invite the very responses guaranteed to make me feel loneliness and fear.

It is through allowing my own vulnerability that I invite those around me to love me, honor me, and recognize my oneness with them. Today I open the gates in front of my heart; may love rush in to find me.

Dear God,

Please remove the walls in front of my heart.
May I see the gentleness in others,
And may they see the gentleness in me.
May Your tenderness
Be my strength
And Your compassion be my guide.

Amen.

My body is a creation of the thoughts I think; I send it love and light.

Today I counter the stresses of the world that would assault my physical body. Throughout the day, I send it love and flood it with God's light.

With every thought I think, I align with the love that heals my body. I cultivate the health of my body by praying it be used as a vessel of God's love. May every cell be infused with light.

Dear God,

I surrender my body to You
And pray it be used as a channel for Your love.
May any impurities in my body or soul
Be washed away by Your divine physician
And neither sickness nor disease remain.

Amen.

Let me not be deterred by the roughness of the road.

The journey to enlightenment is not always easy. Only the darkness I have seen in myself can I then release to God. That process can be painful, but it is pain that leads to peace.

Let me not be deterred by the roughness of this road. Spiritual living is not always quiet, and spiritual relationships are not always easy. I am a pilgrim on my way to bliss, and I will keep in mind the destination of my heart.

Dear God,

Please send Your angels to guide me
As I make my way toward freedom from self.
As my tortured ego cries out in pain
Upon sensing its own demise,
May I be reminded that the death of my ego
Is the birth of my true self.

Amen.

REFLECTION

On Bringing Light to the World

God and man are the ultimate creative team. God is like electricity. A house can be wired for it, but if there aren't any light fixtures, what good does that do? If God is seen as electricity, then we are His lamps. It doesn't matter the size of the lamp, or its shape, or design. All that matters is that it gets plugged in. It doesn't matter who we are, or what our gifts are. All that matters is that we are willing to be used in His service. Our willingness, our conviction, give us a miraculous power. The servants of God bear the imprint of their Master.

Lamps without electricity cast no light, and electricity without lamps casts no light either. Together, however, they cast out all darkness and bring light to all the world.

Let me remember I am complete already.

I need not create the perfect me, for God has already created it. There is no hole that I must fill. I am not lacking, for I am complete in God.

My only need is to remember who I am: a child of God, eternally innocent and changelessly pure. As I align my personality with the truth of my spirit, the light within me then shines through. It is to this process that I dedicate my life today.

Dear God,

Please remove from me
The fears that hide my love,
The darkness that hides my light
And the defects that hide my beauty.
Purify my thinking,
That I might be a reflection on earth
Of the love that is divine.

Amen.

I do not shrink from the pain of transformation.

My ego would prefer I avoid my pain, and not look too closely at the root of its cause. Today I choose the courage it takes to look honestly at who I've been, how I've behaved, and how I've contributed the problems that beset my life.

A moment of crisis can be a moment of growth, as the wounded self prepares to transform. From the chrysalis of my pain, I will forge my healing—the wings of my newborn self.

Dear God,

I am preparing to be a better me,
Facing ways in which I have not been
The person You would have me be.
Be with me as I endure the pain
Of my own humiliation
And emerge forgiven
By You and by me.

Amen.

Instead of anger,
I choose love today.

My anger is a tantrum of my frightened self, like a child in need of love that I alone must provide. I cannot expect anyone else to see the pain beyond my anger. It is my responsibility to soften my behavior.

Indulging my anger is an act of self-sabotage, as it pushes away the very love I need. Today, if I am tempted to anger, I will pray for a miracle to set me free. I am committed to love as the way to heal whatever it is that has thrown me off course.

Dear God,

Please take away my anger,
For it is not an expression of my true self.
Show me the love
That lies beyond it,
And help me show it to others.

Amen.

Today I communicate
with love and grace.

Whenever I'm seeking to express myself to others, I am responsible for my effect. It is my responsibility, and only mine, to communicate in such a way as invites others into my heart.

I am aware that there are ways to speak, and ways to behave, that cause fear instead of love to rise up in those around me. It is not the job of others to figure out who I really am; rather, it is my job to make it clear for all to see. If I want others to see the love in me, then I must show it to them.

Dear God,

Help me hone my personality
So that my love is clear to all,
My softness is hidden from no one,
And my goodness is always expressed.
Help me always find a tender way
To communicate my thoughts.

Amen.

REFLECTION

On Giving Back to God

God has given me my identity, and that cannot be taken away.

God has imbued me with infinite potential, and that cannot be taken away.

God has provided me with the opportunity to change my thinking in any instant, and that cannot be taken away.

God has given me the capacity to love, and that cannot be taken away.

God has entrusted me with the power to live in the light of His abundance in any moment, and that cannot be taken away.

God has given me all those things. I ask myself today, now what shall I give back to God?

I deepen my devotion
to love today.

It isn't the breadth of my influence, but the depth of my devotion, that determines my value to the world. As I deepen my search for God, hastening my journey to love, I affect the world from beneath the level of things that are visible to the mortal eye.

I seek vertical reach into the things that matter most. For thus I will be changed within, and have greater value to myself and others.

Dear God,

I search for You in all things today.
May I hear from everyone the call for love
And see in everything the love that is there.
May my inner eye be opened
To the world beyond the world
That I see with my physical eyes.

Amen.

I embrace each moment as an opportunity for a miracle.

Infinite opportunity is built into the nature of the universe. It is not lack of opportunities, but rather the ways I have deflected them, that has obstructed the flow of miracles into my life.

Today I ask God to take away all things that tempt me to deflect my good. May I not act from my wounds today, but rather may this day be a day of my healing. May God remove my defects of character and replace them with the characteristics of my immortal self.

Dear God,

Please remove from me
All falsity and illusion,
That I might be a shining example
Of a person
Set free from fear.

Amen.

I place all problems in the hands of God.

No matter what my problem, the perfect solution exists within the Mind of God. My job is not to be burdened by the question, but rather to make myself available to the answer. My worrying only delays the answer, reflecting my lack of faith that there is one. Today I will be still, knowing every answer, every healing, and every solution is on its way.

The universe is self-correcting, and I am a child of the universe. Miracles occur in response to every problem, yet it is my faith and compassion that bring them forth. May my mind be a conduit of love and faith, that my problems may be solved.

Dear God,

In You lies the answer to every question
And the solution to every problem.
I place my anxious mind
In Your care
And pray for the calm through which
I can receive Your answers.
And so it is.

Amen.

I place my sadness in the hands of God.

Only in feeling my sadness can I learn from it and deepen through it. My sadness is often my teacher, as I learn to outgrow its causes within myself.

I will not anesthetize myself today, or distract myself from the pain of seeing what is difficult to see but important to look at. Rather, I will look with open eyes on the things I have done to attract my sadness, and commit myself to changing them.

Dear God,

Please remove my sadness
By removing its causes.
Reveal to me what I need to see
That I shall be sad no more.

Amen.

REFLECTION

On the Lord's Prayer

Every single moment, the universe is ready to begin again. The only time that God's time intersects with linear time is in the present moment; miracles happen not in the past or future, but *now*. Every instant, God is pouring forth His love for me, with endless opportunities for renewal and rebirth. God is always saying, "Here is the glory of the universe. Do you want it? Embrace it, for it is yours."

So we say unto all eternity, moment after moment after moment: God, who dwells in the realm of Truth, may your Word be all-powerful in my mind. May the world I live in here on earth reflect the reality of love. May I think Your thoughts, and make manifest Your thoughts. Today, may I receive what I need. May my way be unblocked, as I unblock my heart to others. And when I'm tempted by fear, may I be guided back to loving thought. May love be my experience, power my happiness and peace, in every single moment of my day.

Our Father, who art in heaven, hallowed be Thy name. Thy kingdom come, Thy will be done, on earth as it is in heaven. Give us this day our daily bread; and forgive us our trespasses, as we forgive those who trespass against us. And leave us not in temptation, but deliver us from evil; for Thine is the kingdom, and the power, and the glory, forever and ever. Amen.

Today I will expect less from others, and more from the universe.

Today I will not grasp at people or things I feel I need in order to supply my good. Rather, I'll remember that in God I already have everything.

As I allow all people and things to be, whomever and however they are, the universe will respond positively to my correct positioning of heart and mind. As I allow all things to be, all things will in turn be wonderful.

Dear God,

Please take away my grasping nature.
May my mind not seek to control
Either people or events,
But rather may I look with love on all things.
Then and only then will my world transform
From darkness to light
And fear to love.

Amen.

I am not at the effect of other people's opinions.

God has created me good, and in His eyes I am beautiful. If others cannot see my beauty, it is not that it isn't there. I, like everyone, am good at heart.

As I remember my innocence and have faith in my goodness, I shall not be swayed by the beliefs of others. While others may project their shadows onto me, in truth I dwell in light. I cleave to God today, that I might see myself as He sees me. May His view of me, and His guidance, be the beacon that I follow.

Dear God,

Though others may be convinced
  of my guilt,
May I remember the innocence
  in which I was created.
It is Your light
And Your counsel
That I seek to guide me.
Please remind me who I am.

Amen.

Today I feel my body brilliant.

I have a body of flesh, and a body of light—a body of my mortal self, and a body of my eternal self. Today I feel my body brilliant, created by God, and the home of my true being.

Every cell is filled with light. Neither disease nor compulsion can penetrate the shield of God's blessing upon me. My holiness is the key to both my mental and my physical health. I am lifted above the body of my sorrows and delivered to my body of joy.

Dear God,

I surrender my body to You.
Transform each cell into love and light,
That nothing but Your perfection
Can live within me.

Amen.

When I am internally still, chaos cannot move me.

As I enter any worldly chaos from a place of internal peace, my stillness works to dissolve the chaos. I need not fear any turmoil in the world, as long as there is peace in me.

God's eternal peace is the ground on which I stand, as I navigate the shifting sands of time. The world is always changing, but God within me is changeless. I am loved, I am safe, I am blessed, and I am protected. As I look upon others and wish them those things, I will experience them in myself.

Dear God,

May my mind know Your peace
And never waver.
May my heart know Your love
And never deviate.
May I find myself in You
And You express Yourself through me
No matter what occurs.

Amen.

REFLECTION

On a Self-Organizing Universe

The universe is both self-organizing and self-correcting.
The invisible hand that makes our heart beat and our lungs breathe is at work on multi-dimensional levels, arranging not only the extraordinary physical processes that keep us alive but also what we experience: insights, relationships, improbable meetings, creative moments, falling in love, emotions, and miraculous occurrences.

The universe, in fact, is one miracle after another, one stroke of genius followed by another stroke of its genius in an endless flow of opportunity for life to fulfill itself. And nature is not limited to the so-called natural world. It's as much a stroke of genius that you're sitting next to whom you're sitting next to on the bus today, as that your liver is purifying your blood. The universe is intentional. It doesn't do anything by accident.

The difference between the so-called natural world, and you and me, is that you and I can say "No." The embryo doesn't have a choice whether or not to become a baby; the acorn doesn't have a choice whether or not to become an oak tree; the bud doesn't have a choice whether or not to become a blossom. But you and I do have a choice whether or not to allow life to fulfill itself through us. And the choice we make then determines not only who we will be in the world but also the experiences we will have here.

May all my encounters be holy.

Today I view every encounter as a sacred one, blessing anyone I meet or even think of. May a holy light shine forth from my heart and bless all living things. May my presence on earth be a touchstone for God's love.

I place my relationships in the hands of God, and pray that they be used by Him.

May anyone who enters my presence feel the healing balm of peace. May my thoughts and actions extend the love that fills God's heart, and mine.

Dear God,

Please use my encounters
To increase Your love.
May they be a blessing
On all involved.

Amen.

Today I release all unimportant things.

I will not be affected by a world that exalts the meaningless. I claim my mind for the light of Truth, making it impenetrable to assault by the unimportant.

I do not allow my time today to waste me, or be wasted. I pray for the mental and emotional discipline to notice and to act on only what's important. May I overlook the rest.

Dear God,

Please send Your angels
To guard my mind
And keep at bay
All meaningless thoughts.
I devote this day to meaningful things
And serve them with all my heart.

Amen.

It is not what I do, but rather
who I am, that determines
the quality of my life.

I center myself on the love in my heart, that I might be as a beam of light to whomever I meet and wherever I go today. I need not worry what to do or what to say, for the spirit of my true being will guide my thoughts and actions.

My highest function and greatest mission is simply to be in any moment the person I am capable of being, extending the love of God through me to all the world. Thus I will shine and be radiant and feel the joy of my true self.

Dear God,

I surrender to you
Myself today,
That I might find and be
Who I really am.

Amen.

Everything that occurs today is part of God's plan.

Everything that happens is part of a mysterious educational process in which I'm drawn to situations that constitute my greater learning. I choose in every situation today to be a more beautiful version of myself, so I may learn through joy.

I am invited to play life at a higher level—to be strong where I have been weak, to be healed where I have acted from my wounds, to give love where before I have withheld it. Thus shall this day serve the purposes of God at work in my life.

Dear God,

I surrender all that happens today,
Every encounter and every occurrence,
To Your purposes in myself and others.

Amen.

REFLECTION

On Cancer as Metaphor

A cancer cell is a cell that has gone insane. It has disconnected from its natural intelligence. It has forgotten that it's here to collaborate with other cells, that it exists to serve the healthy functioning of the system of which it is part. It has separated from the organ to which nature has assigned it, gathering other cells as sick as it is to build its own kingdom in a world apart. This false kingdom, this malignant tumor, seeks to preserve itself by growing more of itself. Thus, it threatens not only its host but also itself.

This is not simply a description of cells in the body. It is a description of the emotional malignancy of the human race, which has separated itself from our natural intelligence. This emotional malignancy threatens the whole of humanity, just as the disease of cancer threatens one body. Our disease is the false belief that we are separate from each other, from God, from the rest of life, bearing no sense of responsibility or love for anyone or anything other than the selected beneficiaries of our kindness. This distortion of our true sense of self is a cancer that would lead to the destruction of our species. It tempts us to forget our function as collaborators with others in promoting the healthy functioning of the whole of which we are a part. It will be healed, in our bodies and in our world, as we return to our natural selves.

May I participate in God's work today.

Today I do not look for ways that life can serve me, but rather for ways that I can serve life. I place myself in service to God's endless creativity, praying to be the pencil with which He writes and the paintbrush with which He paints.

May all that is the work of God be furthered by my choices today. I put aside my search for little things and participate freely in the glory of creation.

Dear God,

May my thoughts and actions
Help further today
A work that is greater than my own.
May all I am
And all I do
Be a channel for all things good.

Amen.

Today I choose the light, and turn away all darkness.

I know there is a force within that lures me toward the light, and yet there is a competing force that would keep me bound to darkness. May the love of God cast out the fear that has lodged inside my consciousness, for truly there is no contest when love has power and fear does not.

My choice for God increases His power to dissolve my fear and suffering. Today I choose to live in the light of forgiveness and love, that the darkness of fear shall fall away.

Dear God,

May my mind today be filled with light
So darkness cannot enter here.
May love so saturate my every thought
That fear cannot remain.

Amen.

I will not resist
my growth today.

How often it seems easier to resist the call of a greater be-coming, remaining within the dark cocoon of a self that has settled for good enough. I choose not to remain at good today, but rather to answer the call to greatness.

Not every lesson feels fun while it's happening, and at times I have resisted growth fiercely. But I remain open today to the miracle of transformation, and know that as I forge ahead into a new realm of being that love itself will aid my progress. Spirit will erase the patterns of fear that have sabotaged my past.

Dear God,

Overcome the fear that would keep me bound
And deliver me to the highest heights.
I am ready and willing to forge ahead.
I know that You alone
Can unbind my feet.

Amen.

Today I give birth
to my higher self.

Today I choose my strength and not my weakness, my spirit and not my ego, to guide me on my way. I look to love and not to fear as the light upon my path.

Today I choose the way of the enlightened self, that enlightenment might come to me. I will try my best to walk the softer way, and allow my heart to lead.

Dear God,

May Your spirit
Be born into the world today
Through who I am and what I do.
May Your energy move through me,
And may others feel it too.

Amen.

REFLECTION

On Making Love the Bottom Line

The probability vectors for the next twenty years are disturbing. Humanity is like the Titanic headed for the iceberg, whether the iceberg is weather catastrophe brought about by global warming, nuclear disaster brought about by our reckless use of nuclear energy, or shortage of food or water supply. If looked at only through a rational lens, it could be argued that in all probability, one way or the other, our goose is cooked.

But we have more than a rational lens through which to look, for a spiritual perspective broadens not only the quality of our perspective but also the quantity of our choices.

That is the invitation of this moment in history: to step out of the confines of the limited, mechanistic, fear-based thinking that now dominates our civilization. The human race has reached a crossroads: continue to think and act as we have been thinking and acting, thus reaping the consequences of a loveless, reckless way of being; or break through to the highest calling for life on earth: to make love our new bottom line, thus creating the miracles that will save us from our own self-destructive ways.

May I not lose sight of love today.

We inhabit the world we choose to see; may I not lose sight of love today. If I read about war, may I also remember the possibilities for peace. If I see someone suffer, may I not forget how many people I can help. May hope and faith in possible tomorrows inform my view of today. I will see the fear, but work for love. And fear will fall away.

May I remember today the realm of love that lies beyond the worldly veil, and not be drawn into the illusions of suffering that dominate the earth. My heart remains open to the suffering of the world, but also to its joy. Thus shall I be a bringer of joy, in knowing it is always there.

Holiness is my refuge today.

I gain power in a world that is moving too fast by learning to slow down. The life I want will not emerge from electronic speed but rather from a holiness within me. Then, and only then, will I experience the world as a place that reflects my soul.

I seek the quiet of God's presence today, regardless of what worldly turmoil surrounds me. First in the closet of my inner self, and then as I walk through my day, I will seek and remain within the holy space.

Dear God,

May Your cloak of holiness
Surround me today
And warm me from within.
May the warmth of Your presence
Deliver me from the coldness of the world.

Amen.

May only the love in
my past remain.

May I not be at the effect of past hurts today. I forgive myself and others, and open my heart to the miracle of new beginnings. May the universe rewrite the script of my life, as I allow God's love to purify my mind.

May only the love in my past remain, and all else fall away. May others think of me with mercy, forgiving my transgressions as I forgive them theirs. May we all be released from the chains of our former selves.

Dear God,

I place my past in Your hands.
Please purify my thoughts about it.
May I only remember the love I gave
And the love that I received.
May all else burn away
In the alchemy of forgiveness.

Amen.

Today I believe in miracles.

Even in the midst of my darkest night, I sense the presence of angel wings. Confronted with the limits of what I can do, I realize the limitlessness of what God can do. When the world is at its worst, the miracle of God's love is still ablaze within my mind.

I will not be tempted today to doubt God's power. No matter what occurs today, I know a miracle is possible. I cleave to this knowing and to the power that it brings.

Dear God,

May I not forget Your power,
In my life or in the world.
May Your miracle
Be ever present in my mind.
May I remember that in You
There is always hope.

Amen.

REFLECTION

On Becoming Who We Really Are

Practice kindness, and you start to become kind. Practice discipline, and you start to become disciplined. Practice forgiveness, and you start to become forgiving. Practice charity, and you start to become charitable. Practice gentleness, and you start to become gentle.

It doesn't matter whether you're in the mood to be gracious to the bank teller today; do it anyway—and watch how it begins to affect your mood. Just push the button of the self you wish to be, and the synapses that make up that personality begin to form. Your best self already exists in the ethers, just waiting to be downloaded. We become gracious when we decide to be gracious. We have the power to generate as well as react to feelings; to hone our personalities as we travel through life. In the words of George Eliot, "It is never too late to be what you might have been." It is never too late to become who we really are.

I surrender my
financial fears today.

In God, there is no lack; there is only abundance. In God, there is no meaningless pursuit; there is only endless creativity. In God, there are no endings but only the start of new beginnings.

I dwell in God, that I might be delivered—from the realm of lack, from the pain of meaninglessness, and from the sorrow of perceived failure. I am lifted above the limits of the world to the endless abundance of the Mind of God. And thus I need not fear.

Dear God,

I place in Your hands
My financial concerns.
As I abundantly give of myself,
May abundance be given me.
May I gift the universe
And the universe gift me
In an endless cycle of love.

Amen.

I hear the calling of the ages today.

I hear the calling of the ages today, to make of this world a glorious place. I pray to be used in the precious task of perfecting an imperfect age. May all that I am and all that I do be a harbinger of good.

May I not be deceived by temporal appearances, but live instead in the realm of the eternal. May I thus be a conduit for greater possibility, for myself and others, now and always. Surely the future will be abundantly blessed if we envision it now as a beautiful thing.

Dear God,

I surrender the future to You
And pray to be in service to its most
Beautiful manifestation.
May my ears be filled with the call of the ages
And my actions be guided to serve it well.

Amen.

I find my own self-esteem
by esteeming God.

In exalting God, I myself am exalted. As I live in service to a higher truth, I am delivered to a higher place. Only in seeking to give praise to God, do I find that I am praised.

My smaller self is not the light of the world. Rather, it is the spirit within me that lights up the universe. It is to God that all praise is due, for who and what I am in my light-filled place.

Dear God,

All praise and thanksgiving
To the light You are,
And the light in me,
Which is the light we share.
May I identify
Only with You,
That I might know who I truly am.

Amen.

I am not a body.
I am a child of God.

Not my body, but my spirit, is who I truly am. My mortal self is not my total self, but rather a fraction of my being. I accept today that I am part of God, therefore a part of the immortal world.

My body is but a temple space. May it serve me well in extending light from my spirit into the world. My body is blessed as I see it correctly, as a device for giving love.

Dear God,

May my body serve Your purposes
As a conduit of love.
Deliver my cells
From darkness
To light
And my being
From false to true.

Amen.

REFLECTION

On the Key to Happiness

It seems to me that the key to happiness lies in getting over ourselves. The happiest times of my life have been when I was more involved in something I was doing for others than in something I was doing for myself. For any perception that focuses only on our separate needs will ultimately breed fear, and any perception that focuses on our oneness with others breeds peace. Many people struggle and fail to find peace within themselves, because they don't really realize who their "self" is. That is why the ego is so dangerous: it would have us believe that we are separate, when in fact we're not. We can't have inner peace unless we feel complete within ourselves, and we can't feel complete outside our connection with other people.

You cannot find yourself by only looking to yourself, because in essence that is not where you are. The real you is an expanded self, literally one with the entire world. And so we find ourselves in unity with others. We cannot be happy unless we are wishing everyone the same.

My work for God
is effortless.

Ego struggles, but spirit creates with effortlessness and joy. I rise above the burden of work, as I give what I do to God. It doesn't feel like work to work for love.

Angels push me from behind today, and guide my thoughts and actions. I relax into the flow of love, allowing myself to float upon the waves of a cosmic sea. I release all resistance that I might experience accomplishment and joy.

Dear God,

I surrender to You
My worldly efforts.
May I know not tension
But joy,
As I am carried by the flow
Of love.

Amen.

I allow my dreams
to live today.

I will not deflect, diminish, or invalidate my dreams today, or concoct excuses for why they can't happen. However outrageous they seem to be, I allow them to live within me. Today I will not limit my dreams.

I honor the images of my deeper self, and invite them to reveal to me the meaning of their message. I make a space within the temple of my mind for God, the Dreamer of All of Life, to dream His dreams through me.

Dear God,

May I not be restricted by my mortal mind,
For in You all things are possible.
May I not be limited by the thinking of the world,
Or by the illusions of time and space.
May the dreams
That You would dream through me
Be not blocked by thoughts of fear.

Amen.

The purpose of my life is to grow into my perfection.

The embryo needn't struggle to become a baby, and the acorn needn't struggle to become an oak tree. Nor do I need to struggle to become the person I am created to be.

I am supported by nature in the process of my self-actualization. As I show up in glory, my life will be glorious. As I celebrate the beauty of life, life itself will celebrate my beauty. As I relax into the flow of the miraculous, then miracles will find me. I will embody in time the perfection of my true self.

Dear God,

I surrender to the thoughts of love,
That I might find my way to You.
In finding You, I will find myself,
And then I will know joy.

Amen.

I trust that it is
safe to love.

Knowing my defenses merely bring to me that which I defend against, I release my barriers to love today. It is my defenselessness that ensures my safety. I need not fear love, for God's wisdom guides my thinking about everyone and everything.

Within the space of love, I own my "yes" and my "no," both my gentleness and my firmness. I trust God's guidance to reveal to me where I should and should not be. I trust that it is safe to love.

Dear God,

I place in Your hands
My thoughts about everyone and everything.
Please give me wisdom
And give me strength.
Show me what I need to see,
That I might always remain in light.

Amen.

REFLECTION

On Shedding Light

There is a way of being in the world that transcends the world, a way of being regular people and miracle-workers at the same time. We become the lamps that shed the light that emanates from the electricity of God. No one feels deeply at home on this plane; it is not where we come from, and it is not where we are ultimately headed. It is a place we stay but for a little while, beautiful and blessed when we allow our perceptions of it to be overshadowed by His, but a way station nonetheless. We are here because we have a mission: to be the love that is missing in a loveless world and thus reclaim this darkened world for light.

I seek a bigger life today.

I cannot live in fear and expect great love. I cannot be narrow-minded and expect the world to open up to me. I cannot experience my full potential unless I'm willing to take risks.

Today I pray for courage. I surrender the attitudes and behavioral patterns that keep from me my greater good. I am willing to be a bigger person, that I might have a bigger life.

Dear God,
Please remove the fears in me
That keep a fuller life at bay.
Interrupt the patterns of weakness
I have inherited from former times.
Deliver me to my greater self.

Amen.

Every moment holds the possibility of endless possibility.

Creation itself is a thing of love, and where there is love there are always miracles. Anything is possible where there are no impediments to love.

No matter what illusions of the world may rage, I believe in the possibility of infinite possibility. Miracles are built into the nature of the universe, and I am open to receive them. May love prevail in myself and others.

Dear God,

Please work the impossible
Where a miracle is needed.
Please bring forth love
Where fear is rampant.
Please pave a way beyond all darkness,
And show the light to me.

Amen.

May I see myself
as God sees me.

God created me a perfect creation, and so in spirit I remain. May the light of my internal perfection cast out any darkness in my mortal self. Thus may I express in the world the love that is in my heart.

May God's opinion, and not the opinions of others, determine how I see myself. May God's thoughts, and not my own, determine what is possible for me. May my self-perception rest only on the vision that God holds of me.

Dear God,

Please lift me above the shadows
Of my negative self-perception.
Please deliver me of the chains
That keep me bound to a smaller life.
Please show me the beauty
You have placed in me,
And give me faith that it is there.

Amen.

Today I seek to do one thing that interrupts a pattern of fear.

Today is the day of my release, as I declare myself free of the bondage of the ego. I will do one thing, however small, to forge a path of greatness where I have formerly cowered in fear.

I need not repair every aspect of my wounded self today. Rather, I need only practice the thinking and behavior of a greater good. With this, I build new pathways in my brain and in my life.

Dear God,

Please free me of the habits
That keep me bound
To a life I don't wish to live.
Break the chains that hold me back
From claiming my greater good.
I will try today.
Please help me.

Amen.

REFLECTION

On Seeing Ourselves
as God Sees Us

We can have in life whatever we are willing to be. For ultimately, being and having are the same. When we grant ourselves permission to live the life we want, there is little in the world that can stop us. Our weakness is often simply a weakness of faith—believing more in the limitations of the world than in the limitlessness of God. In fact, there is no limit to what's possible in our lives. God does not just think—He knows—we are unlimited beings, because that is how He created us. Our task is to learn to see ourselves as He sees us—totally light, totally loved, and totally empowered.

The universe is pregnant with ever greater plans for me.

There are times when nature gathers up its forces, outwardly calm but inwardly busy preparing for its next great move. Such is true in the world and in me.

Today I remain calm in the inner knowing that great things are being prepared for me. I prepare my heart for what is to come, receiving with graciousness the beauty of a future beyond what I can imagine.

Dear God,

I thank you in advance
For all the miracles in store for me.
May my heart be open
To receive Your blessings.
Then may they extend through me
To bless the entire world.

Amen.

What I appreciate appreciates.

Today I appreciate all the blessings in my life. I do not take for granted all the wonderful things I have. I feel my gratitude with a humble heart.

I appreciate my abundance. I know that as I do so, my abundance will increase. May all that I have be used by God to bless others as it blesses me. I am reminded of those who live lives of pain, and pray to be useful to heal their suffering.

Dear God,

Today I give thanks for all I have.
All that it is, I surrender to you
And pray it be used for a greater good.
And so it is.

Amen.

Today I will speak
from my heart.

When I speak from my mind, others hear me with their minds. When I speak from my heart, others hear me with their hearts. Today I will speak from my heart.

There are no limits to the blessings I receive when I speak with love and gentleness. May I not be tempted today to choose fear or anger as the mode through which I express myself. Rather, may I remember that to do so is to sabotage my good.

Dear God,

Please make of me
An instrument of Your peace.
May my words reveal Your tenderness
And my heart express Your love.

Amen.

Every situation is a lesson that God would have me learn.

Every situation is a lesson to be learned—a lesson in being a kinder person, in becoming more excellent, in lifting my circumstances higher. May I see everything that occurs today as an opportunity to step up my game.

In this way I will know the joy of spiritual growth. May every encounter be a holy one, every circumstance be a platform for a miracle for myself and others, and everything I do today be a glorification of God.

Dear God,

I give this day to You.
May it serve Your purposes
And increase Your good
In the world.
May every situation in which I find myself
Take me closer to You,
And thus to who I really am.

Amen.

REFLECTION

On the Limitlessness of God

To God, every moment is a new beginning. And God is held back by nothing. God would never say, "I could help you, but you messed up badly so I don't want to." Neither does He say, "I could give you a great life, but your parents were dysfunctional so my hands are tied." Limitations do not stand before the limitlessness of God; it is only the limits to our faith, not the limits of our circumstances, that keep us from experiencing miracles. Every situation provides us the chance to live with broader, more audacious hope and faith that all things are possible. God is bigger than any limited circumstance in our past; God is bigger than any limitation that the world is showing us now. Limitations exist only as a challenge to us to mature spiritually, as we realize that through the grace of God we are bigger than they are.

Bigger than financial lack? Yes, because in God you are infinitely abundant. Bigger than sickness? Yes, because in God you are in total good health. Bigger than terrorism? Yes, because in God we are infinite love, and love is the one and only force that hate and fear cannot withstand. There is no order of difficulty in miracles. If enough of us pray each morning, asking God to send His spirit into the messes we've created and make all things right, surrendering our own ideas and asking for His instead—then all our problems will begin to dissolve.

Today I empty my mind and ask God to fill it with His thoughts.

Enlightenment is not learning but unlearning. Today I release my attachment to the filters through which I view the world. I accept instead that the only true filter is love.

All that the world has taught me, I surrender to God. May His spirit purify all my thoughts, and release me from the guilt that dominates the mortal plane. May I only see innocence in myself and others, and may all else fall away.

Dear God,

I surrender all thoughts of guilt.
I pray instead to see only innocence
In myself and others.
May my mind be an empty container
To be filled by You and You alone.

Amen.

Today I surrender my weaknesses and pray that they be healed.

I am aware of my character defects today. I know God is merciful, and wills that they be removed not through suffering but through joy. Today I pray to be shown a better way to live, that my wounds might be healed and my defects removed.

I accept responsibility for looking clearly and honestly at who I am and what I do. I know God walks with me through this thorny path of self-discovery. He does not guide me to suffering but to release from suffering, as He shows me the love I have hidden before and teaches me how to express it.

Dear God,

I release to You my weaknesses and wounds,
My fears and defects.
Please remove them all,
That I might be a pure expression
Of who You created me to be.

Amen.

I choose to be a
miracle-worker today.

When centered in an attitude of blessing, I am an automatic miracle-worker. A palpably more positive atmosphere prevails when I reach for the highest within myself. I will try with every thought to embrace love instead of fear.

Others will feel energized and uplifted along with me, as I rise to the holiness within myself today. When tempted to judge, I will withhold my judgment. When tempted to attack, I will lay down my sword. When tempted to display the energies of my lower mind, I will choose instead to display my truth. And thus miracles will occur.

Dear God,

Help me today
To choose love over fear,
That I might work miracles
For myself and others.
Where I am tempted
To attack or defend,
Please guide my mind
To a gentler place.

Amen.

May my relationships serve God's purposes.

Relationships are laboratories of the spirit, or playgrounds for the ego. They can be heaven or they can be hell. They are infused with love or infused with fear. Which they are for me is my choice.

My ego would use relationships to serve my needs as I define them, as it tries always to compensate for what I think I lack. In truth, the purpose of my relationships is that I and another experience maximal growth and joy. Such are the purposes of God.

Dear God,

I place my relationship with _____
In Your hands.
May my presence be a blessing on his life,
And may he be a blessing on mine.
May my thoughts toward him be those of innocence and love,
And may his toward me be the same.

Amen.

REFLECTION

On the Meaning of Life ❦

When we were born, we were programmed perfectly. We had a natural tendency to focus on love. Our imaginations were creative and flourishing, and we knew how to use them. We were connected to a world much richer than the one we connect to now, a world full of enchantment and a sense of the miraculous.

So what happened? Why is it that we reached a certain age, looked around, and the enchantment was gone?

Because we were taught to focus elsewhere. We were taught to think unnaturally. We were taught a very bad philosophy, a way of looking at the world that contradicts who we are. We were taught that we're separate from other people, that we have to compete to get ahead, that we're not quite good enough the way we are. We were taught to see the world the way that others had come to see it. It's as though, as soon as we got here, we were given a sleeping pill. The thinking of the world, which is not based on love, began pounding in our ears.

Love is what we were born with. Fear is what we have learned here. The spiritual journey is the relinquishment—or unlearning—of fear and the acceptance of love back into our hearts. Love is the essential existential fact. To be consciously aware of it, to experience love in ourselves and others, is the meaning and the purpose of our lives.

I place my relationships
on the altar to God.

The ego speaks first and the ego speaks loudest. It will always make the case for separation: someone did this or that and therefore does not deserve my love. In any moment I listen to the ego—denying love to another—then to that extent I will be denied. I pray for a power greater than my own to push back the storm of my neurotic thinking. What I place on the altar to God is then altered within my mind.

My relationships are part of a divine curriculum designed for me by God. I invite His spirit to enter my mind, that my thoughts might be guided to innocence and love and not stray to defense or attack. In that way, my relationships will be blessed and their potential for love fulfilled.

Dear God,

May my relationships be lifted
To divine right order
And take the form
That best serves Your purposes.
May all unfold,
Within me and the relationship,
According to Your will.

Amen.

In giving to others,
I give to myself.

In the spiritual universe, we only keep what we give away.
Many thoughts that masquerade as self-interest are actually
thoughts of self-sabotage. When I think about myself at the
expense of others, I am subconsciously seeking to deny myself.

Surrendering to the ways of God is not an act of self-sacrifice,
but rather the opposite. For in withholding from God, withholding my love, I am sacrificing a life of spiritual abundance
and emotional freedom. Today I give my love to others, that I
might feel more loved.

Dear God,

May I not be tempted
To withhold my love.
In surrendering to love,
I surrender to the force
That wishes for me my greatest good.
The ego speaks, but the ego lies.
May love drown out its voice today.

Amen.

May I not be lost in a meaningless world, but rather find myself in the love of God.

The meaningless thoughts that dominate the world infect my consciousness when I allow them to, dragging me down into the bottomless wells of anxiety and despair. We are not left alone in such painful places, for God has sent His spirit to save us from the darkness of the world.

Today I remember that pain is not real, but the product of illusions created by meaningless thoughts. I pray for God to guide my thoughts beyond fear, to the love within His Mind and mine.

Dear God,

Reach out Your hand to me
In my despair,
That I not sink into
The hell of my own making.
Show me who I really am,
That I might rise
Above the illusions
Of my fearful mind.
Deliver me to love.

Amen.

I don't ask God to change my circumstances, but to change who I am within them.

We're all assigned a piece of the garden, a corner of the universe that is ours to transform. My corner of the universe is my own life—my relationships, my home, my work, my circumstances—exactly as they are.

I don't ask God to change my circumstances, but to change who I am within them. May I tend every part of my garden with love, that it might grow to be the most beautiful manifestation of all that is good, holy, and true.

Dear God,

Make me the person
You would have me be,
That I might do what You would have me do.
Make of my life the most beautiful thing
By reminding me who I am.

Amen.

REFLECTION

On Reclaiming the
Knowledge of the Heart

Meaning doesn't lie in things. Meaning lies in us. When we attach value to things that aren't love—the money, the car, the house, the prestige—we are loving things that can't love us back. We are searching for meaning in the meaningless. Money, of itself, means nothing. Material things, of themselves, mean nothing. It's not that they're bad. It's that they're nothing.

We came here to co-create with God by extending love. Life spent with any other purpose in mind is meaningless, contrary to our nature, and ultimately painful. It's as though we've been lost in a dark, parallel universe where things are loved more than people. We overvalue what we perceive with our physical senses, and undervalue what we know to be true in our hearts. It's time to reclaim the knowledge of our hearts, that the world might be set free.

My life is made new today.

Today I stand for radical change, within myself and in my life. My future is reprogrammed in this very moment as I allow God's spirit to enter here.

Nothing is needed in order for this to happen, except the free flow of love from my heart.

Today I pray for a miracle. I shall allow it to happen, and not resist it. I am open to a new beginning, a life unlike the past. My relationships shall be made new. My career shall be made new. My body shall be made new, and my mind shall be made new. Not later but now, not elsewhere but here, not through pain but through peace. And so be it.

Dear God,

I affirm with all my heart
That in You
All things are made new.
May my mind and body,
Relationships and attitudes,
Reflect the alchemy of Your miraculous power
In me and all beings.
And so it is.

Amen.

I let go my grievances, that I might have a miracle instead.

A ny guilt I see in another will blind me to my own per-fection. Today may I see the innocence and love in others, even when they've presented to me the darkness of their egos. May I be released from my own darkness, as I stand willing to see past theirs.

Those we need to forgive are our most important teach-ers, for they indicate the limits to our capacity for forgiveness. Where there is a grievance, there cannot be a miracle. Today I let go my grievances that I might have a miracle instead.

Dear God,

I give to you
My grievances,
That I might have a miracle.
May I be released from my own guilt
As I release others from theirs.
May I see the innocence beyond the mistakes
In my brother and in myself.

Amen.

Now is the instant of
my salvation.

The only thing to be saved from is my own neurotic thinking, and salvation is found in any moment when I rise
above it to embrace God's love. Every instant, I have a chance
to change both past and future by reprogramming the present.
I dedicate today to the miracle of living fully in the present.

May I remember each instant today that I am on this earth
for one reason only: to love and be loved. May every thought
be illumined by the remembrance of my cosmic function, and
my behavior be guided by its wisdom.

Dear God,

May my mind not be clouded today
By confusing thoughts that lead me nowhere,
Unimportant things that block the truth,
Or fears that hide my love.
Every instant, may Your spirit remind me
Of who I am, who others are,
And why we all are here.

Amen.

I am willing to endure the discomfort of self-discovery, in order that I be healed.

As I ask God to heal my life, He shines a light on everything I need to look at. I see things about myself that perhaps I'd rather not see. Like everyone, I have armor that has accumulated in front of my heart—often masquerading as something else.

I am willing to face the truth about myself and all the games I play, for I know God goes with me—not to punish me but to heal me. I am willing to endure the sharp pains of self-discovery, in order to release the dull pain of unconsciousness that could otherwise last for the rest of my life.

Dear God,

I surrender to You
My fear and my resistance to finding out who I really am.
I am willing to understand myself,
That I might serve You more.
Please send Your angels to accompany me
As I journey through the jungle of my fears
To the meadows of peace beyond.

Amen.

REFLECTION

On Reclaiming Our Power

Love requires a different kind of "seeing" than we're used to—a different kind of knowing or thinking. Love is the intuitive knowledge of our hearts. It's a "world beyond" that we all secretly long for. An ancient memory of this love haunts all of us all the time, and beckons us to return.

We want to return, because we want our power back. Love provides us with a "second sight," an ability to discern the meaning of things that lies beyond facts alone. It gives us a greater astuteness regarding human personalities, and a deeper understanding of events beyond their surface appearance. Love doesn't mean we give up a power; love is how we reclaim it.

Today I accept that I am whole and complete.

While I know that God created me perfect, I do not always feel that way. I know my sense of self is fractured, and I am willing to be healed. Today I accept myself as God created me, so I might experience the truth of who I really am.

In places where I doubt myself, or feel insecure, or feel in whatever way that I am not enough, I ask God's healing of my self-perception. May I be lifted above the false sense of self that would lead me to conclude that I am less than who I am. May I remember that as a child of God, I am whole and complete and shall remain that way forever.

Dear God,

Please heal my fractured sense of self.
I am prone to feeling flawed,
Not good enough,
Or otherwise less than you created me to be.
I need a miracle to set me free
Of my false beliefs about myself.
Thank you, God.

Amen.

I will remember today that ultimate reality is always perfect.

Behind gray clouds there is always blue sky; behind the veil of illusions that dominate the world there is always the truth of eternal love. That which is eternal is the truth of who we are—changeless, loving, and immortal.

I will not be swayed today by the appearances of the world. I will not be tempted into despair. For I remember that the suffering of the world is a product of our collective madness, and God has promised to heal us. I surrender my mind for healing today, that I might be part of the mass awakening that is lifting all of us out of our nightmares.

Dear God,

May I not be tempted today
To believe in the illusions
Of suffering and loss.
May I rather see through them to the possibilities for healing
And be used by You to bring the healing forth.
And so it is.

Amen.

My disappointments are but temporary setbacks.

At any time there might be an occurrence in which mistakes occur and sorrow results. Yet for any wrong turn there is an automatic recalibration within the Mind of God. I need only be patient and wait for a perfect universe to make right again any paths that have gone wrong.

I will not allow my emotions today to fall into the valley of defeat because of a temporary setback. And all setbacks are temporary. My salvation lies not in an immediate change of circumstance, but in my ability to remain positive and optimistic during times of duress. God is the answer to every problem the moment the problem occurs, and I await cheerfully the miracle that is always on its way.

Dear God,

I surrender to You
A situation that disappoints,
And pray to be shown any aspects of my thinking
That helped cause my sorrow.
Undo the consequences of any false beliefs
That put the universe at odds with my joy,
That thus I may be happy again.

Amen.

I rejoice in all that is good.

Today I will not fail to notice the miracles of life unfolding around me. From beauties of nature to the gentle power of forgiveness, I stand in awe before the creations of God.

Whenever my mind focuses on a problem in the world, I will still remember that babies continue to be born, people continue to fall in love, forgiveness still works miracles, and where there is love there is always hope. I consciously recognize today all the amazing gifts of life. I will try to be conscious of even the tiniest demonstrations of the miracle of life.

Dear God,

May my eyes be opened wider today,
That I might see more
Of Your awesome creation.
May I not be tempted to focus elsewhere
Than on the truth of You.
Even when I bear witness to that which is wrong,
May I remember that in You there is always a way
To make things right.
And so it is.

Amen.

REFLECTION

On Invoking Love

People who are always telling us what's wrong with us don't help us so much as they paralyze us with shame and guilt. People who accept us help us to feel good about ourselves, to relax, to find our way. Accepting another person doesn't mean we never share constructive suggestions. But like everything else, our behavior is not so much the issue as the energy it carries. If I'm criticizing someone in order to change them, that's my ego talking. If I've prayed and asked God to heal me of my judgment, however, and then I'm still led to communicate something, the style of my sharing will be one of love instead of fear. It won't carry the energy of attack, but rather of support. Behavioral change is not enough. Covering an attack with sugary icing, with a sweet tone of voice, or therapeutic jargon, is not a miracle. A miracle is an authentic switch from fear to love. When we speak from the ego, we will invoke the ego in others. When we speak from love, we will invoke their love.

I bless all the children in the world today.

I take this day to recognize the beauty of children and our responsibility toward them. Their beauty, their sweetness, their vulnerability, their love—may their needs as well as their preciousness be foremost in my mind.

May I not forget the relative powerlessness of children to represent their needs as the world goes on around them. Those who have no families to care for them, to nourish them, to love and sustain them are the responsibility of all of us. May I never be blind to either their beauty or their needs.

Dear God,

Please bless the children of the world.
May their tender emanations
Awaken the heart of all adults.
May their needs be moved
To the forefront of our consciousness
And the world reorient itself around them.

Amen.

Today I use prayer to call forth miracles for everyone.

Anyone I see today, I remember to silently bless him or her. Anywhere I go, may my presence bring forth love. I will silently pray today for the happiness of everyone.

I remember today that prayer is a force, a medium of miracles, a power beyond what the world believes. I pray as a way of harnessing God's love and using it to work miracles in the lives of others. As I do so, I too shall be blessed.

Dear God,

I pray for all beings in the world today . . .
For the happiness of all,
The peace of all,
The healing of all.
I pray to be a person
Who makes a difference somehow
And helps heal the world.

Amen.

I trust that God has a perfect plan.

I trust there is a perfect plan for the unfolding of my highest good, which my rational mind cannot perceive or formulate. God's plan works, and mine does not. I cannot know how my part fits best into a larger plan for the healing of the world, but God does. My job today is merely to open my mind and open my heart so that a higher consciousness can then flow through me.

I know I am not alone in a random universe, but rather I'm held safely in the arms of God.

Dear God,

I put my trust in You,
To lay a path before me
Leading from darkness into light.
In every moment that I am aligned with You,
Your plan is at work in me.
May I cleave to what is true,
That the truth shall ever guide me.

Amen.

Today I walk forward in the confidence God provides.

I do not need to create myself, or make myself worthy. For all of us are perfect creations of God. I need only allow the light within me to shine forth for others to see.

I do not lack confidence, for I am confident in God who lives within me. I am neither better nor worse than anyone else, and in that lies my freedom to love and be loved.

I need neither to add nor to subtract from my essential being, for whom God has created me to be is more than enough. I walk forward today in perfect confidence that the holiness within me, created by God, is the truth of my being and the light of the universe.

REFLECTION

On Communicating with Love

Miracles are created in an invisible realm. The Holy Spirit improves our style. He teaches us how to communicate from love instead of attack. Often people will say, "Well, I told them. I really communicated!" But communication is a two-way street. It only occurs if one person speaks, and the other one can hear them. We've all been in conversations where two people spoke and no one heard a thing. We've also had conversations where no one said anything and both people understood everything perfectly. In order to truly communicate, we must take responsibility for the heart space that exists between us and another. It is that heart space, or the absence of it, which will determine whether communication is miraculous or fearful.

I seek to be who I am capable
of being, that I might do what
I am capable of doing.

Divinely inspired being precedes divinely inspired doing. I seek to be today who God would have me be, that I might know—and be capable of manifesting—that which He would have me do.

As I make the focus of my attention the enlarging of my compassion and the honing of my gentle self, then all I am meant to do will proceed from who I have chosen to be.

Today I call forth my highest mission, by standing in the space of my highest self. As I do so, the universe arranges itself to pave the way for my highest performance in the world. I will naturally attract all people, all ideas, and all situations that make it so. Amen.

May my work become my ministry.

I change the purpose of my work today from a job to a ministry. A job is merely an exchange of energy, while a ministry is the platform for my highest service. It is the place from which I serve. I am not on earth just to do a job; I am on earth to fulfill the spiritual mission of becoming God's light and love on earth.

Whatever I do, I can do with an attitude of service. Whatever I do, I can do as a way to serve the world. As I dedicate my work to higher purposes, my work shall be lifted, transformed—and even exchanged for other work, if necessary—to serve God's plan to use my talents for His sake.

Dear God,

I surrender
My talents and abilities
For the purposes of love.
May my work become my ministry,
And all I have and do be used by You.
Thus shall I experience the joy
Of knowing
That what I do is for a higher cause
Than my mortal mind can know.

Amen.

Today my path
unfolds before me.

As I become who I am meant to be, what I am meant to do will fall like a path of rose petals before me. I may not feel I know what my path is, but God does. He knows how my talents and abilities can best fit into His plan for the enlightenment and healing of all things. What talents I have, He will glorify as I use them to glorify Him. And talents I don't even know that I have, that lie latent within me, will emerge as I surrender more deeply to love.

Talents that lie latent within me will arise as I surrender my heart. They will take form as I begin to view everything I do as a way to serve God and to serve the world.

Dear God,

Please pave another path before me
Than the one that I have tread.
As I change my mind,
Please change my future.
Fill my mind with love,
That only love might lie ahead.

Amen.

Today I answer God's call.

Today I dedicate to an active listening to the voice of God within me. May I hear His call to open my heart, and heed not the voices of fear. Thus His voice shall proclaim through me the emergence of a better world.

As I hear God's call within me, I answer with all my heart. Our love will resonate throughout the universe, and form the calling of my soul on earth. Great power will emanate from this greatest of loves. And so it is. Amen.

REFLECTION

On Seeing We Are One

Our needs are not separate, because all of us are one. What I think about you, I will think about myself. And what I see in myself, I will see in you. Only by accepting our oneness, do we come to see our differences in the light of truth.

On the level of spirit, there is no place where you stop and I start. Like waves in the ocean or sunbeams to the sun, there is no real separation. Separation does not actually exist, for there is only one of us here. The thought of separation is the illusion at the core of all problems in the world. As I heal my own thoughts of separation, I contribute to its healing everywhere.

Today I choose to learn
from my failures.

A failure remains a failure only if I refuse to learn from it. Any situation that teaches me greater humility, sobriety, wisdom about self and others, responsibility, forgiveness, depth of reflection, and better decision making—teaching me what's truly important—is not an ultimate failure. Sometimes what I deem a failure at the time it happens actually serves to foster a change within me that creates an even greater success down the road.

Great people are not those who have never fallen down. Great people are those who, when they do fall down, dig deep within themselves and find the strength to get back up. Today may I be someone who rises from the past.

Dear God,

I feel that I have failed.
I feel that all my efforts have come to naught.
I feel shame at the way my life has turned out.
Please, dear God, repair my heart, heal
  my mind, and change my life.
Pave a way for me out of darkness into light.
I atone for my errors and I pray for forgiveness.
Please do for me what I cannot do. Thank you, God.

Amen.

God is constantly creating
through me.

God, as love, is constantly expanding, flourishing, and creating new patterns for the expression and attainment of joy. When my mind, through focus on love, is an open vessel through which God expresses, my life becomes a canvas for the expression of that joy. That is the meaning of my life. It is why I am here.

I wasn't just randomly thrown onto a sea of rocks. I have a mission—to help save the world through the power of love. The world needs healing desperately, like a bird with a broken wing. People know this, and millions have prayed. God heard us. He sent help. He sent each and every one of us to do His work on earth.

Today may I be a canvas on which God Himself can write, a vessel through which He can operate His miraculous authority on earth. I open myself to receive His power that it might then extend through me, as a blessing I receive and then a blessing that I give.

May God make every
decision for me.

Basing my decisions on the matters of the world should be balanced with weighing them against the matters of the heart. Once legalities, medical opinions, accounting, and other people's perspectives have been factored into my thinking, I will remember to place all ultimate decisions in the hands of God. I know the most powerful way to make any decision is to ask God to make it for me.

Then I will know through the auspices of my heart what my mind alone could never discern. Spiritual forces will then move on my behalf.

Dear God,

Please make this decision for me.
I do not see the future,
But You do.
I do not know what's best for everyone,
But You do.
I cannot make sense of this,
But You can.
Dear God,
Please decide this for me.

Amen.

May I actualize the Light within me.

Everyone I meet, every situation I find myself in, represents a lesson that would lead me to the next step in the actualization of my true self. Everything that happens is part of a mysterious educational process in which I'm subconsciously drawn to the people and situations that constitute my next assignment. With every lesson I'm challenged to go deeper, become wiser and more loving. And whatever my next lesson is, it awaits me wherever I go.

God's work is the work of my greater becoming, and I don't have to be somewhere else, or doing something else, in order to do it. Right in front of me, on this very day, there are things to do and thoughts to think that represent a higher "possible me" than the one I have been manifesting. In any given instant, there is more love I could express.

Today may I expand the boundaries of my capacity to love. May I be more forgiving, more merciful, more compassionate, and kinder. May others feel in my presence more permission to shine, as the light of God shines through me to bless them and lift them high.

REFLECTION

On Success

Success means we go to sleep at night knowing that our talents and abilities were used in a way that served others. We're compensated by grateful looks in people's eyes, whatever material abundance supports us in performing joyfully and at high energy, and the magnificent feeling that we did our bit today to save the world.

Our work should spread love. Our store should spread love. Our technology should spread love. Our business should spread love. Our life should spread love. The key to a successful career is realizing that it's not separate from the rest of our lives, but is rather an extension of our most basic self. And our most basic self is love.

Today I choose
to think with love.

Crossing the bridge to a better world begins with crossing a bridge inside myself, from the addictive mental patterns of fear and separation, to enlightened perceptions of unity and love. I have been trained by the world to think fearfully, and today I choose to think with love.

To achieve a miraculous experience of life, I embrace a more spiritual perspective. Otherwise, I will die one day without ever having known the real joy of living. I am committed today to seeing everyone and everything as part of God's plan for me, and for them. May everyone I see and everything I do be used by my higher mind as a lesson in love. May fear thus dissolve in my presence and lose its grip on my life.

Today I command fear to go back to the nothingness from whence it came, as I embrace the love that alone casts it out of me. I choose love, I embrace love, and I cleave to love. Though I know I shall be tempted by fear, I also know I shall be saved by God and delivered to the peaceful shores of love given and received.

The universe is infinitely abundant, and so am I.

The universe is infinitely abundant. As a child of the universe, I am entitled to the miracles that flow forth from it freely. Yet though the orchard is filled, I must reach for its fruits. Today I make myself miracle-ready by recognizing I am entitled to the miracles of love.

While the material world is a kingdom of lack, the spiritual universe is infinitely abundant. As I identify with the spiritual kingdom, my mind becomes a vessel through which I receive its riches. I am open today to receiving the abundance that is part of who I am.

Today I recognize that I am entitled to the riches of the universe. I am never denied abundance by God. His will is that I receive His plenty, that I might then extend it into the lives of others. Lack and struggle are not of God, and I am part of Him.

I am confident in who I am because I know God lives within me.

The true me, my holy self, is beyond any limits of the mortal world. As God lives inside me, so does His brilliance and infinite power. As I dwell in that knowledge, recognizing and appreciating His divine spirit that resides in all of us, I receive the charisma of a self-confident person.

Confident in God, I am confident as a person; seeing myself as God's follower, I come across as a leader in the world. I live within an invisible light, a sense of humble certitude, and a greatness that comes from beyond myself.

God's greatness lives within me, creating ever-more-expansive patterns of life and love. It sings to me, and I sing back, a continuous song, from my heart to the universe and the universe back to me.

Every encounter is a holy encounter.

My goal today is to give and receive love, which is another way of saying, "May God's will be done." Today I see every interaction as a holy encounter, in which love is the true bottom line; may I be within each encounter the best person I can be.

I intend that every situation be one in which I express my truest, most loving self. What happens beyond that, I leave to the intelligence of the universe. I'm not going anywhere to get anything, but to give my all. I'm not going into an interview, for instance, to try to get a job; I'm going there to do my job!

Dear God,

May my presence today,
Wherever I am,
Be a blessing on all beings.
May my expression, my words and my actions
All align with Your divine will.

Amen.

REFLECTION

On Changing Your Mind

If you think of yourself as being at the effect of a random universe that does not care about you, then you will experience your life that way. If you think of yourself as being at the effect of a loving universe that does care about you, then you will experience your life that way.

No matter what is happening in our lives, we choose how we wish to think about it. And the greatest gift we give ourselves is often our willingness to change our minds. Despite what might seem to be the saddest and most intractable situation, we have the power to believe that something else is possible, that things can change, that a miracle can happen. This gives us vision, which gives us conviction, which gives us power.

If I cower from my greatness, I withhold from the universe.

Unlimited potential lies within me, waiting to be activated by my readiness to express it. Knowing this, I am a magnet for worldly success. As I work from joy, the world will respond with joy. As I open my heart, the way will be made clear for me.

Such owning of my power is an affront to my ego. But I take a stand for my greatness today, that the ego shall fall away.

I will not be tempted by false humility today. Rather, I remember that it is humble, not arrogant, to receive and express the power of God. The power of God is unlimited everywhere, including within me.

In order to go deep, I make sure I go slowly.

When things in the world are troubling, my need is not to join in the chaos but to cleave to the peace within. The way to gain power in a world that is moving too fast is to learn to slow down. The only way to spread one's influence wide is to learn to go deep. The world I want for myself will not emerge from electronic speed but rather from a spiritual stillness that takes root in my soul. Then, and only then, can I create a world that delights my spirit instead of one that shatters it.

Dear God,

May I remember to go deep in each moment,
To truly see and hear and reflect
On what is happening all around me.
May the depth of my vision and the clarity of my perceptions
Then deliver me
To a peaceful place.

Amen.

Today I bless the world.

As I wake up today, I bless the world. I pray to be a servant to something holy and true. I breathe deeply and surrender myself to God's plan for my life. I devote this day to miracles.

Working miracles is the calling of my soul, the call to leave behind the thoughts of fear and replace them with the thoughts of love. Fear is dying away, in me and in the world. And love is upon us all, if I allow it within me.

Love is tender but love is strong. The meek shall inherit the earth for one reason only: their strength will literally take the place over. Today may the meekness within my soul become a powerful force in my life.

Today I make love more important than things.

Often I have gotten things that I thought would make me happy, only to find that they did not. This external searching—looking to anything other than love to complete me and to be the source of my happiness—is the meaning of idolatry. Money, sex, power, or any other worldly satisfaction offers mere temporary relief for minor existential pain.

When I attach value to things that aren't love—the money, car, house, prestige—I am loving things that can't love me back. I am searching for meaning in the meaningless. Material things, of themselves, mean nothing. It's not that they're bad; it's that they're nothing.

Today I will not look to nothingness for an experience it cannot give me. I look to love, to connection, to beauty, and to forgiveness to satisfy my soul. As I do so, I will find there a peace that the material world cannot bring. And from that place, I will dwell more peacefully in the world.

I detach from any false beliefs that the material world is the source of my good. I embrace instead the understanding that it is only in the discernment of meaning that I can find my solace. I find inner peace as I detach from the belief that the outer world is my salvation.

REFLECTION

On Enlightenment

You are loved, and your purpose is to love. From a mind filled with infinite love comes the power to create infinite possibilities. We have the power to think in ways that reflect and attract all the love in the world. Such thinking is called enlightenment. Enlightenment is not a process we work toward, but a choice available to us in any instant.

Enlightenment is the answer to every problem. In any situation where you seem to be at the effect of forces over which you have no control, remember that God dwells within your mind, and there are no forces over which He has no control. Therefore, through His power within you, there are no mortal conditions over which you are powerless. Whenever your good is obscured by the appearances of an unloving world, the universe is programmed to lift you out of that condition and return you to an abundant state.

Today, *how* I do things is as important as *what* I do.

Everything I do is infused with the energy with which I do it. I know that what I'm feeling is communicated subconsciously to everyone, and every thought I think creates form in some way.

Taking responsibility for my energy is as important as taking responsibility for my behavior, and today I will do that. I seek in any situation to be a blessing, a miracle-worker, an expander of love. That is my only goal, that I might experience true peace.

Every thought, every feeling, every action has consequences beyond what we can see. I pray today that the emanations of my mind and heart be purified of fear and uplifted to the level of divine right order. May I thus be an instrument of peace.

I am willing to look at what I need to look at.

Having asked God to heal my life, I know a light will shine on things that I need to look at. I might see things about myself that I'd rather not see, and today I commit to myself that I will not look away.

Light cannot be poured over darkness, but rather darkness must be exposed to the light. Otherwise, it merely festers. I am willing for my darkness to come to light, that I might surrender it to God and pray it be taken away.

Dear God,

I surrender to You
My darkness.
Please pour forth Your light upon it.
May all I am be brought to You
And purified of fear.

Amen.

Today I choose
to stand on faith.

My mind is never faithless, for faith is an aspect of consciousness. I either have faith in the power of fear, or faith in the power of love. It seems easier at times to have more faith in the power of my problems than faith that they can be miraculously solved. Today I choose faith in love.

Faith in a positive outcome doesn't mean I'm denying a problem; it means merely that I'm affirming a solution. Where I put my faith directly influences what happens next.

Dear God,

May I always remember that Your invisible power
Is at work in all things.
May my faith in the realm beyond this world
Overcome my fear and transform my thinking.
May I thus invoke the evidence
That my faith was well placed in You.

Amen.

I recognize
the power of prayer.

Prayer changes my life by changing *me*. It places me on a different ground of being within myself. It gives me confidence in a power that is in me but not of me, that can do for me what I cannot do for myself. It keeps me from sinking into victim consciousness—a stance that attracts more victimization—and lifts me to positivity, that I might attract more positive outcomes.

I commit to prayer this day as my primary problem-solving method, placing my thoughts about all things in the hands of God. I surrender my mental filter in favor of God's, asking only to see through the eyes of love.

I pray for happiness for myself and others. I pray to be an instrument of peace. I pray for a greater capacity to forgive. I pray for the well-being of all. I pray that love prevails. Amen.

REFLECTION

On Divine Compensation

As an expression of divine perfection, the universe is both self-organizing and self-correcting. To whatever extent your mind is aligned with love, you will receive divine compensation for any lack in your material existence. From spiritual substance will come material manifestation. This is not just a theory; it is a fact. It is a law by which the universe operates. I call it the law of divine compensation.

Just as there are objective, discernible laws of external phenomena, so there are objective, discernible laws of internal phenomena. The law of gravity, for instance, is not just a "belief." It is true whether or not you believe it. Spiritual laws are not just beliefs, either; they are descriptions of how consciousness operates. Once we know this law—that there is a natural tendency of the universe to improve all things—then we lean naturally into the arms of God and allow Him to lift us up. We surrender our thoughts, then He uplifts our thoughts, then our experiences change.

I am more sensitive to the pain of others today.

Often we ignore the suffering of others—not just those who cry out in pain, but also those who suffer silently around us. May I be more sensitive today to those who could use a kinder word, an encouraging embrace, a sensitive listener to their story.

How clear we are that we ourselves are sensitive, while too easily forgetting that so is everyone. Today may I be a person who leads with kindness, who listens well, and displays a generous heart. May everyone I meet today be blessed by my presence.

Dear God,

Today may I not forget
That I am only here to love,
To heal the heart of the world,
And to forgive the illusions
Of myself and others.
Make me an instrument
Of a greater good.

Amen.

I do not shrink from the power God gives me.

I am on this earth to extend God's power, not shrink from it. For God is the power of love. In Him and through Him, there is nothing I cannot achieve. I am on the earth to seek His will for me and to carry out His guidance.

It is not my power, but His, that moves through me as I surrender myself to the authority of love. I pray to be used for higher purposes than my own, and know I will be sent on tasks that only God could choose for me. My path is blessed and my success guaranteed.

Dear God,

I stand in awe before Your majesty
And in gratitude that You have chosen me
Through which to express Your glory.
May my mind be lifted
To higher heights
Wherein Your power lies,
That I too might be magnificent.

Amen.

Today I bless those I am tempted to judge.

In denying love to anyone, I deny myself a miracle. In withholding forgiveness from anyone, I withhold it from myself.

Today I think of someone I am tempted to judge, to blame, to criticize, and I remember he or she is a child of God. If any of us are beloved by God, then all of us are beloved by God. May I see all beings through the eyes of God, that I might know their innocence and mine.

Dear God,

Whom I am tempted to judge,
You do not judge.
May I see them as You do,
That I might judge no more.
May I see beyond the veil of guilt,
Focusing no more on the mistakes of others.
May I see instead the light of innocence
That is the truth of who they are.

Amen.

I take responsibility for the power of my mind today.

The power of God is within us. We can misuse this power, but we cannot obliterate it. Whether our hearts are open or our hearts are closed, with each thought we express the creative power of the mind. Whether to heal or harm, we attest to the power within us. May all my power be used for good today.

With every thought, I manifest form on some level. With every thought, I bring forth either love or fear. May I be ever conscious of my power today, in how I think and how I behave.

Dear God,

May Your spirit overshadow my mind today
And purify each thought of the ravages of fear.
May the thinking of the world not tempt me away
From the thought of love that is who You are.

Amen.

REFLECTION

On Meeting Limits with Unlimited Thought

Our power lies in meeting limited circumstances with unlimited thought. It is not what happens to us, but what we choose to think about what happens to us, that determines what will happen next.

If our circumstances tempt us to think thoughts such as, "I'm such a loser," "I will never have another chance," "It will take forever for this situation to right itself," or "I hate whoever is to blame for this," then miracles, though they are programmed into the nature of the universe, cannot make their way into our awareness. They're in the computer, but we're not choosing to download them. With every thought we think, we either summon or block a miracle.

It is not our circumstances, then, but rather our thoughts about our circumstances, that determine our power to transform them. We choose in life whether to live in victimization or in victory. We have power either way—power to use against ourselves, or power to use to free ourselves. The point is that we always have the choice.

I am fully present for my life today.

Every moment carries within it the seeds of new beginnings, of miracles, of infinite possibility. Only my own lack of presence and awareness can keep those realities from my door.

Today I will show up for life. I will be the best that I can be. I dedicate my life to the good, the holy, and the beautiful. I will not waste my life today.

May I not be held back today by illusions of lack, obsessions about meaningless things, or thoughts of fear. May the love that is in my heart blaze forth, creating miracles for myself and everyone. May I be fully present for my life today, that my presence might bless the world.

My power in the world will emerge from the power in my heart.

My power doesn't lie in my résumé or connections. My power doesn't lie in what I've done or even in what I'm doing. My power lies in my clarity about why I'm on the earth. My desire to serve God will create the means for me to do it.

God can use the flimsiest résumé. He can use the smallest gifts. Whatever my gift to God, however humble it may seem, He can turn it into a mighty work on His behalf. My greatest gift to Him is my devotion. From that point, all doors will open.

Whatever I do today, whatever effort large or small that I exert on behalf of healing the world, can be turned into a mighty work. I dedicate my efforts—my work both personal and professional—to be used by God. I will be amazed by what He then brings forth.

I know that salvation is only found in the present.

The only point where God's time, or eternity, intersects with linear time is in the present moment. As I live fully in the present, I transcend all neurotic thoughts about past or future. Past and future are only in my mind, and they are purified as I release them into the hands of God.

Today I am saved from obsessions about past or future, the regrets over what was or what might have been, and the grasping for a future I cannot control. My salvation lies in relaxing into the arms of God in each and every moment, safe and secure in the realization that this moment is all that is real.

Dear God,

Please save me
From the endless torment
Of attachment to past or future.
Send Your spirit
To heal my mind
Of the temptation to enter the nothingness of time.
Keep me firmly in the present,
Where I know I am blessed.

Amen.

I will not shirk my responsibility to look deeply into myself.

Ego would prefer that I not look directly into my deeper self, for there I would learn things bound to free me from its bondage. I would learn of the endless beauty that lies beyond the writhing of my personal self. I would learn that beyond my torment lies the glory of my soul.

Today, I choose a conscious life. I will ask myself when something has not turned out well, "What did I do or not do that helped cause this to happen?" Only then will it be revealed to me the source of my pain. I will be healed as I am willing to look honestly at myself.

Dear God,

Send angels to accompany me
On my path to self-awareness.
May embarrassment not deter me
From looking at the truth of how I behave,
For only when I see my patterns
Will I be able to change them.
Please take from me the shadows that
   would hide Your light in me.

Amen.

REFLECTION

On Choosing Faith

Faith is power. It changes your life by changing you. It places you on a different ground of being within yourself. It gives you a confidence based on something that's in you but not of you, that can do for you what you can't do for yourself. It keeps you from sinking into victim consciousness—a stance that attracts more victimization—and lifts you to positivity, which attracts more positive outcomes. Where we put our faith literally and directly influences what happens next.

I can have faith in the power of the world, or faith in the power of miracles. I can have faith in the power of fear, or faith in the power of love. I can have faith in the power of external things, or faith in the God who lives within me.

Today I communicate
with love and not fear.

The word "communication" includes the word "commune." If I communicate without communing, I do not communicate at all.

I am responsible for the heartspace between me and whom I communicate with. If someone feels attacked or judged or blamed by me, they will not hear me. I might speak but I will not have been heard. Today I will find the innocence within myself and others, the place of holy communion, before I speak. Then not only what I say, but how I say it, will be heard as a sharing and not an attack.

Dear God,

Please help me communicate
With love and not fear.
Let me assure whomever I speak with
Of their essential goodness,
Even if they might have been wrong.
For otherwise, I will be wrong myself.

Amen.

Love can be trusted.
Without love, I am insane.

Love makes all things right, by aligning mortal events with the natural patterns of an intentional and creative universe. Love is my *sanity*. It does not lead me into unreasonable or immoderate behavior. It is the guidance system for a wise and peaceful life.

The thinking of the world would lead me to believe that the ways of love are often ways of weakness, while the ways of fear are often ways of strength. Never has a more insane perspective taken hold of the human mind. I shall not be lured into the thinking of darkness, but rather I will cleave to love today.

Dear God,

When the world
Would lay its lies upon me
And tempt me to perceive without love,
May Your angels guard my mind
And keep me firmly in Your light.

Amen.

God has assigned me a function that only I can fill.

Each of us has a unique part to play in the healing of the world. Each of us is assigned by God a function that only we can fulfill. At the level of our divine function, none of us are in competition with each other, for the universe is infinitely abundant.

My good doesn't take away from anyone else's, and no one else's good takes away from mine. There is space for *everyone's* gifts to flower. There is more than enough room for all of us. I embrace the assignment revealed to me when I open my heart to love.

As I seek to live as God would have me live, He will reveal to me what He would have me do. He will prepare me in all the ways I need, to carry out the role He would have me play. I need only to relax into His presence within me, and all shall unfold in divine right order. Amen.

God's greatness is a gift
that I humbly receive.

God's greatness is a gift that is offered me, and it serves Him when I receive it. I have latent power that is mine to claim. I often lack faith in *what* exists within me because I lack faith in *who* exists within me.

Today I accept with gratitude and humility the presence of God within me. I am a vehicle for the ecstatic power of grace, always ready to move through the veins of my consciousness and my body. God's greatness is the antidote to the suffering of the world.

God is great, and God is within me for God is in my mind. I surrender my thoughts of brokenness and fear, to be replaced by endless love. Thus shall I receive the gifts of God and extend them to the world.

REFLECTION

On Accepting Our Calling

One of the most positive transitions you can make is from viewing your work as a job to viewing it as a calling. A job is an exchange of energy in which you do a material task and someone provides money in exchange. A calling, however, is an organic field of energy that emerges from the deepest aspects of who you are. It is the fulfillment of what God has created you to be and do. Approaching your work as a job versus approaching it as a calling makes all the difference in whether or not you dwell in the miraculous universe.

You have a calling simply because you are alive. You have a calling because you are a child of God. You have a calling because you're on this earth with a divine purpose: to rise to the level of your highest creative possibility, expressing all that you are intellectually, emotionally, psychologically, and physically in order to make the universe a more beautiful place.

As you do this, your entire life becomes your ministry—a way to serve God and to serve the world.

Forgiveness works miracles.

In any moment, I choose where to put my focus. I can focus on someone's guilt, or I can focus on someone's innocence. By seeing someone's innocence, I transcend the effects that their guilt might have had on me.

I am only at the effect of what I accord reality. By forgiving, I accord reality to love, and therefore only love can touch me. Through forgiveness I let go of fear, to work a miracle instead.

The power of forgiveness is a miracle of God, a shift in perception from world to spirit, from past to present, from fear to love. It is God's greatest gift to me and my greatest power. My willingness to forgive is my refuge, my security, and my strength.

I let go of my attachment to the pain of my past.

Often it's said we can be bitter or we can be better. Today I choose not to be bitter, for my bitterness will create more reasons to be so. As I rethink my past, forgiving myself and others, I release myself from the damage of old wounds.

My clinging to old hurts might inspire sympathy for a time, or even temporary support from others. But it will not inspire invitations to start over, from other people or from the universe itself. I can have a grievance or a miracle; I cannot have both.

I place my grievances in the hands of God, and pray for deliverance beyond my attachment to bitter wounds. I let go of my grasping at what I cannot change, and pray for a miracle to release me from my pain. I surrender all thoughts of judgment and revenge, that I might now be free.

I will not punish myself for the mistakes of my past.

The dark nights of my soul have taught me many things: about where I got it wrong and where I got it right in life; about who I've been and who I choose to be now. I take responsibility for my mistakes, I atone for my errors, I do what I can to make things right, and I allow forgiveness and mercy to wash me clean.

It neither serves me, nor anyone else, for me to continue to beat up on myself. Having burned through appropriate remorse, I wish to move ahead and grow from my mistakes. I will not stay stuck in the mire of self-hatred. Although I have made mistakes in my past I am not bound by them in the present—for my atonement is sincere. God Himself would not have me punish whom He Himself has forgiven.

Dear God,

Please help me accept Your mercy and forgiveness.
May I be as kind to myself
As You are to me.
May I begin again
With a heart that's clean of the guilt
I would lay upon myself.

Amen.

I release my character defects to God.

I know there are parts of me—how I think and behave—that are dysfunctions embedded in my personality. I feel shame when I see them, yet I will not look away. I see them and I atone for them. I release my character defects and pray that God take them away.

I know my defects are not where I am bad, but rather where I've been wounded. But regardless of the events that led to their development, I am fully responsible for my defects now. I accept what they are, surrendering them to God with a prayer that He pave a new path in my consciousness. Thus shall I, and those around me, be free of who I used to be.

Dear God,

Please take from me
The things I do that deviate from love.
I surrender the thinking
That binds me to dysfunction,
And pray that Your spirit come upon me
And change me.
Return me to my essential self
That I might be in all ways
Who You created me to be.

Amen.

REFLECTION

On Surrendering to God

Surrendering a situation to God means surrendering your thoughts about it. You're programming your mind to think thoughts that are the most creative, positive, insightful, and beneficial. You're not giving up responsibility or turning your power over to something outside yourself; you're taking the highest responsibility for your circumstances, asking God to make your mind a literal touchstone for miraculous breakthroughs. You walk forward in the confidence that God provides.

Surrender makes way for a larger sense of self—not the false self, but the true. It's an expansion of our realization of who we are when we allow our minds to merge with the field of the divine. Dropping our sense of physical boundaries, we are open to the totality of our existence. In our emptiness, we find our fullness in God.

I break free of the thought
of limits today.

Today I break free of a belief in limits, as there are no limits in the Mind of God. There is no order of difficulty in miracles. The universe is a field of quantum possibility, wherein nothing limits what love can do.

I do not bow before the ego's dictates of scarcity and lack. Rather, I embrace the infinite abundance of God's universe. I face the world today knowing that anything can happen, for there is no appearance of lack or fear that can prevail upon the will of God. God is love, and fear is illusion. Knowing this, I am a natural worker of miracles and a deliverer of peace.

May I be freed of thoughts of worldly limits today, remembering that the children of God are not bound but free. May God's spirit deliver me beyond the narrow confines of fear-based thinking. May I be delivered to the infinite possibilities of love. Break me free, dear God, of the ego's claims of what is possible, what is to be expected, and what is permitted by its harsh assessments of who I am. Amen.

I dedicate myself to love's purposes today.

That which is put in the service of love is protected from the grips of fear. That which is put in the service of deep sanity is protected from the grips of neurosis. That which is put in the service of what is good, holy, and beautiful is protected from the forces of destruction. Today I put my life in service to love.

The ego has no power in the presence of holiness, and my mind is holy. Today I dedicate myself hourly, even moment by moment, to love's purposes, as a way of casting out of my mind the ego fears that would otherwise assault me.

Dear God,

I place all that I am
And all that I have
In Your hands.
Take from me every thought
That is not of You,
And fill my mind
With Your emanations
Of love.
And so it is.

Amen.

I use prayer and meditation to exercise my spiritual body.

Just as I look to food to fuel my physical self, I look to meditation and prayer to fuel my spiritual self. Just as I look to physical exercise to strengthen my physical body, I look to spiritual exercise to strengthen my spirit.

Gravity works on both physical and emotional levels. Just as I do not wish physical gravity to pull down my muscles, I don't wish spiritual gravity to pull down my thoughts. I work against emotional gravity—thoughts of fear, cynicism, negativity, victim consciousness, anger, judgment, and defensiveness—by praying and meditating throughout the day.

The ego will constantly tempt me to attach myself to a fear-based interpretation of the world. I fly instead on angels' wings—the thoughts of love—above the fray of worldly confusion. I pray and meditate to keep my mind on love. And thus I soar above the illusions of the world.

May I hear the voice
for love today.

Today may I hear the voice for God above the voice of the ego. May the calm of love override the chaos of fear in my mind and in the world.

I ask today what I can learn, what insight God would give me, and what wisdom He would place within my heart. May my thoughts be illumined by forgiveness. May love be my touchstone and my salvation from fear. May His voice be with me throughout the day.

Dear God,

May I not be swayed today
By projections of guilt,
By attack and defense,
By limitation and fear.
Rather, may Your love
So fill my mind
That I am utterly calm
Within Your arms.

Amen.

REFLECTION

On Affirming That
Only Love Is Real

In any situation where loves does not rule, affirm that only love is real. Say it, repeat it, chant it like a mantra. Allow it to cast out all thoughts of blame and judgment and fear. Think of the mean-spiritedness of someone, then affirm that only love is real. Watch a horrible story on the news, then affirm that only love is real. Feel your own fears about this or that, then affirm that only love is real. This does not put you in a state of denial, but rather in a state of transcendence. You are not pretending that something is not really happening, but only that it is not *really* happening. No manifestation of fear will long remain once we rise to the realization that only love is real.

Today I choose to be miracle-minded.

Through the authority of loving thought, I am given the power to turn any situation that is not love back into love, by thinking about it differently. Today I choose to be miracle-minded. Where I feel fear, I will choose love. Where I see guilt, I will choose to forgive. Where I fear lack, I will choose to remember that in God all things are possible.

Miracles will intercede for my holiness whenever I choose love, bringing inner light into a darkened world. Today I choose the power of God over the weakness of my ego, to guide me and to set me free.

Wherever there is love, there are miracles. Miracles occur naturally when I use my mind to serve its purposes. Today I am devoted to the work of miracles in myself and in the world. Amen.

Love alone is the meaning of my life.

From infinite love come infinite possibilities. I am loved, and my purpose is to love. I have the power to think in ways that reflect and attract all the love in the world. Such thinking—or enlightenment—is not a process I work on, so much as a choice available to me in any instant.

The world will tell me that my purpose is this or that, my goals should be this or that, and meaning lies in this or that. But love—my ability to give and to receive it—is life's only meaning. Today may I remember that.

God and God alone is the source of my good. Love and love alone is the source of my life's meaning. Forgiveness and forgiveness alone is the key to my deliverance from the pain of a broken heart.

As I let go of the past, I allow for miracles in the present.

My situation might indeed be bleak. I might have made a huge mistake, been given a raw deal, or been betrayed by others. Yet still, what matters is what I think now: Am I lingering in the past, or allowing for a miracle in the present? Am I blaming myself and others, or forgiving myself and others? Am I attached to what happened, or embracing new possibilities?

The universe forges a new path forward, in any instant when I realign my thoughts with the thoughts of love. The laws of time and space are malleable, for through holiness I transcend them. I am entitled to more than help; I am entitled to miracles.

Dear God,

Please wash me clean
Of yesterday's fears.
Let not my attention drag behind
As I enter the light of this holy instant.
Keep me in the present where You reside
And where I belong,
For thus shall miracles be mine.

Amen.

I get rid of my enemies by making them my friends.

The only way out of enmity is through forgiveness. I refuse to allow my grievances to hide the light of God in me. I free myself of judgmental thoughts, for they cause my heart to suffer.

I think of those I blame and send them love. I think of those I resent and wish them well. I think of those who have hurt me and I pray for their happiness. Thus shall spirit infuse my mind, and deliver me beyond the pain of condemnation.

Thinking of every person who has caused me pain, or so I believe; of everyone who has betrayed me, or so I believe; or everyone who is wrong, or so I believe—I now release all blame. I leave to God all efforts to balance the rights and wrongs of anyone, and pray that all of us now be at peace. Amen.

REFLECTION

On Disempowering the Ego

The ego teaches that things like credentials, prestige, money, and worldly power are more important than love. It counsels that we're separate from others, that we have to compete to get ahead, and that we're not quite good enough the way we are. And by our thinking such things, we perpetuate a world in which they seem to be true.

We can escape that world only by changing the thoughts that created it. Such things as credentials, prestige, money, and worldly power refer to our external selves, and our external selves are not who we are. Once we know this, we escape that world. As we begin to realize that we're not here to do any of the things the ego suggests, but rather to love, forgive, serve, and heal, we disempower the ego. For just as the Wicked Witch in the *Wizard of Oz* began to melt in the moment that Dorothy threw water on her, the ego loses all its power when we give all power to God.

Love is what we were born with. Fear is what we have learned here. The spiritual journey is the relinquishment—or unlearning—of fear and the acceptance of love back into our hearts. Love is the essential existential fact. It is our ultimate reality and our purpose on earth. To be consciously aware of it, to experience love in ourselves and others, is the meaning of life.

I release my negative self-concept.

I desire to think of myself as God thinks of me, and to know myself as He knows me. I was created, as was everyone, as divinely perfect. Though I don't manifest my perfection on a consistent basis, my spirit, having been created by God, is perfect nevertheless.

I release any self-concept that fails to appreciate the beauty of God within me. A negative self-perception serves no one, for hiding my own light from my eyes also blinds me to the light in others. I choose to see the light and beauty in everyone, including me.

Dear God,

May I know myself
As Your beloved child.
May I always remember
You created me
In holiness and love.
This is truly who I am,
And so shall I remain.

Amen.

Aging does not diminish my beauty.

Never at any point does the universe give up on me, consider me not good enough, or consider me a has-been. Only if I think of *myself* in such ways do I block the flow of miracles into and through me.

My value does not decline with my physical beauty. As my outer beauty begins to fade, my inner beauty shines forth most brightly. To the universe, I am never invisible.

I realize the light in each of us is the gorgeousness of the universe, no matter our age or physical condition. I live with humble gratitude for the light that shines within me. I will not be tempted by worldly thoughts that would hide from me my value.

I am in touch with my anger, and I release my anger.

I want both to be in touch with my anger and to release my anger. What I do not want is to project my anger onto someone else in the false belief that I will then feel better. Such behavior offers temporary relief, yet a more enduring suffering.

Anger, if I feel it, should be acknowledged. But I need not, and should not, act on it in dysfunctional ways. I feel my anger, accept it is there, and surrender it to God for transformation. May spirit alchemize my broiling emotions, that I might rise above them.

I ask that my anger be transmuted by love, so I might be shown another way to handle my despair. May my anger be replaced by a higher way of seeing. Today I make a stand for my capacity to move beyond my anger, as I place any temptation toward attack thoughts into the hands of God. Amen.

God forgives me, for He never judged me.

G od loves me when I act wisely, and He loves me when I am foolish. His love is based not on how I've acted but on who I am. He knows who I am, for He created me. God's love is unconditional.

My errors do not call for God's punishment, but for His correction. As I atone for my errors—willing to make amends with a repentant heart—then His merciful hand shall reorder events to allow me new beginnings. Such is the miracle of a non-judgmental God, the source of all good and the reason for unending praise.

How awesome is God that—even when I have fallen from grace, from the truth within me, from the love that is the meaning of my life—He loves me still. How merciful is God that—even when I have broken the bond that ties me to His righteousness—He has created the Atonement to allow me new life. My gratitude is deep, and shall forever be. Amen.

REFLECTION

On Meditating in the Morning

Many do yoga or work out in the morning. Many eat breakfast, read the newspaper, and shower in the morning. But those who empower themselves most in life are those who meditate in the morning.

Through meditation, we cultivate our inner strength and release our inner power. We align our spirits with God and place our minds under the direction of divine guidance. We open our hearts to the holy, and greet the day lovingly before sauntering out to meet it. We prepare ourselves as miracle-workers so we can then go out and work miracles.

May my way be unblocked today, as I unblock my heart.

The path before me isn't set in stone, but in my conscious-ness. All fearful thoughts result in fear; all loving thoughts result in love. I unblock my heart today, that I might walk a path of love.

No matter what path I have taken to this moment in my life, I can change it as I change my thoughts. I forgive myself and others; I let go the past and release the future; I remember that there is no limit to the miracles that come from God. Thus am I released from fear, and set upon a path of love.

Dear God,

May my mind not stray from love.
May my heart not stray from love.
May my feet not stray from love.
Not today or ever.

Amen.

May my eyes be opened to the miracles around me.

Every instant, the universe begins again. Miracles happen not in the past or future, but *now*. Every moment, God is pouring forth His love, with endless opportunities for renewal and rebirth. His voice proclaims eternally, "Here is the glory of the universe. Embrace it, for it is yours."

May I not resist the beauty of life, the colors of nature, or the nuances of light. May I not be hardened to the fragility of the heart. May I not abandon the field of miracles that is laid before me every moment of my day.

Dear God,

Open my eyes that I might see
And open my ears that I might hear
The magnificence of everything.
Open my mind that I might know
And open my heart that I might feel
The radiance of everything.
Open my soul that I might realize
The miracle of You.

Amen.

I am who God
created me to be.

I am a child of God. I was created in a blinding flash of creativity, a primal thought when God extended Himself in love. Everything He touches is infused with His wonder, and He has touched me.

The perfect me isn't something I need to create, because God has already created it. The perfect me is the love within me. I allow His spirit to remove the fearful thinking that surrounds my perfect self, so I might extend to all the world the light He placed in me.

May every thought I think and every feeling I feel be an extension of God's love. May fear and illusion fall to the wayside as I embrace the knowledge of who I really am. I am who He created me to be, and nothing else is real.

God and I are one.

God is my source, who continues to fill me with His nurturance and love. I am never without His sustenance, for in every moment He pours into me His divine elixir. Every cell within me opens up to receive His light.

I do not look to outer things to complete me, for I am complete in God. I do not look to outer things to sustain me, for I am sustained by God. I need only to realize who I really am, and my relationship to Him. I live in Him as He lives in me; my God and I are one.

God is closer to me than my breath. He is the light of compassion and the power of forgiveness. He is the truth of my being and the source of my strength. As long as I remember this, I will know who I am.

REFLECTION

On Letting Go of Who We Aren't
So We Can Be Who We Are

When Michelangelo was asked how he created a piece of sculpture, he answered that the statue already existed within the marble. God Himself had created the Pietà, David, Moses. Michelangelo's job, as he saw it, was to get rid of the excess marble that surrounded God's creation.

So it is with you. The perfect you isn't something you need to create, because God already created it. The perfect you is the love within you. Your job is to allow God to remove the fearful thinking that surrounds your perfect self, just as excess marble surrounded Michelangelo's perfect statue.

The great, enlightened beings of the world are those who have done that—who have actualized the spiritual potential that exists inside us all. By following their path, we follow the path that leads to our own enlightenment. Our task is to drop the nonessential clutter that surrounds our shining selves.

Rejection is never
of my true self.

The real me cannot be rejected. If someone doesn't see my beauty, it's not because it isn't there. If someone doesn't appreciate my value, it's not because I'm less valuable. My value—like everyone's—is inestimable because my value is established by God.

No one's opinion can increase or diminish the truth of who I am. May I accept others as God accepts me. May no one feel rejected by me, that I might feel rejected by no one.

May I be lifted above the pain of rejection, as I remember that who I really am cannot be rejected. May God's acceptance mean more to me than the acceptance of any person, for it is based on my true worth. May I always remember, when dealing with someone, to make them feel as accepted by me as I wish to be by others.

Today I will not play small.

Today I will not allow false modesty to keep me from claiming the power within me. God placed it there to be used on His behalf, and I serve no one by hiding my light. Pretending to be less than I am is a game that I play at my peril.

In truth I have only scratched the surface of the gifts I can give to the world, and it is my mission while I'm on earth to give to life all I have. I arrived on this planet with a store of power, and so far I have only allowed myself to experience but a fraction of it. As I devote this power to be used in the service of the healing of the world, it will ignite into a mighty force. Such is who I am.

Today I see the beauty and power and importance in everyone, that I might see it within myself. It is humble, not arrogant, to accept the power of God within me. Nothing in the world can match in importance the gifts that God has given me.

All of us are special and none of us are special.

Every heart is filled with a blazing potential for greatness. Everyone carries the same eternal spark, the same seed of God within us. Everyone is equal at the deepest level of our souls.

Today may I recognize everyone as a brother or sister on my journey through life, struggling as I struggle and yearning as I yearn. May I extend the compassion I wish to feel from others, to everyone I meet. May my eyes thus be opened to the truth beyond the veil.

Dear God,

May I cast no one
Out of my heart today.
May I see everyone as my brother
In light
And my companion along the way.
May I see in all of us
The truth of You.

Amen.

My spiritual journey is the meaning of my life.

Spirituality is an inner fire, the mystical sustenance that feeds my soul. My spiritual journey drives me into myself, to a sacred flame at the center of my being. This journey gives me eyes to see, and the inner strength to live the mystery of the real.

Walking the roads of the outer journey, outside the blaze of mystical truths, I am cold and spiritually lifeless. I am less than my potential when I am lost within the illusions of the world. Today I awake to the world beyond the veil, and find the meaning of my life at last.

May my eyes be opened today, that they might penetrate the darkness of a world that has forgotten love. May my ears be opened to hear the cries of the heart that go out from every soul. May I not be tempted by the thinking of the world to forget why I am here.

REFLECTION

On Remembering Who We Are

We are heir to the laws that govern the world we identify in. If we think of ourselves as only beings of the
mortal world, then the laws of scarcity and death that rule
this world, will rule us. If we think of ourselves as children of
God, whose real home lies in a realm of awareness beyond this
world, then we will find we are "under no laws but God's."

Our sense of who we are determines our behavior. If we
think we're small, limited, inadequate creatures, then we tend
to behave that way, and the energy we radiate reflects those
thoughts. If we think we're spiritual beings with an infinite
abundance of love and power to bring to the world, then we
tend to behave that way. Who we think we are determines
what we do; what we do then determines what we experience;
and what we experience then determines our suffering or joy.
It's hard to overestimate the importance of remembering who
we are.

Today I am a conscious counterforce to the world's despair.

Today is a time of rebirth and renewal. Our world is threatened by an over-identification with the material world. Humanity is called to awaken from an irresponsible stupor, in which we have recklessly forgotten that dictates of love should be central to all we do. Today I commit myself to a path of awakening, that I might be of service to the new.

May all that I do and all I create be of use to God. May my life be in some small way a counterforce to the world's despair. May the products of my mind and the work of my hands bring forth miraculous results for everyone.

Today my life
is radically new.

Today, I choose not to be who I was yesterday. I choose to no longer identify with the darkness in my past. I choose to detach from the drama of former times. I put my life in the hands of God.

Through Him, I enter the radical blessing of new possibilities. My heart is unburdened by the shadows of painful memories, for in God I have new life.

Today I will look inward, not backward, that I might receive the miracle of rebirth. The past is over and lives only in my mind. I forgive myself and others and walk ahead into the light of God.

Today is the day
I have prayed for.

Every day offers me the miracle of life, if I am open to receive it. Everyone offers me the miracle of love, if I am willing to bless them. Every moment offers me the chance to start over, if I am open to its messages to me.

Today is the day I have prayed for, a day of peace and blessing for everyone. God creates only beautiful days. Through Him, may I create nothing less.

Dear God,

May I live up
To Your creative genius
Within me.
May I partner with You
In co-creating a world
Of beauty and blessing
For everyone.
Use me that I might be of use.
And so it is.

Amen.

I do not walk alone through life.

Whatever happens in my life today, I know it is a part of my journey.

If I'm happy, I will not take my happiness for granted. If I'm sad, I will remember that times will change. If there is conflict, I will pray for a miracle. If there is fear, I will pour forth my love.

Every moment is part of a divine curriculum, and I do not wish to avoid its lessons. I open my heart today to the fullness of existence, praying to receive its blessings no matter what they are.

I do not walk alone through life, for God is within me and around me. I am blessed and protected in all I do. Every moment carries a gift for me. May I receive it and pass it on.

REFLECTION

On the Miraculous Authority
of an Awakened Heart

Until we remember that each of us is entitled to miracles, it's easy to despair about the state of the world. If we think of power only in external terms, it's easy to feel hopeless when unjust systems have power.

But when we remember the magic of our inner selves—activating otherworldly forces through devotion and forgiveness and love—we rise to realms of miraculous authority that can, and always do, transcend and cast out the injustices of the world. No external system of tyranny can stand forever in the space of an awakened heart. In the space of light, darkness disappears. In the space of love, fear disappears. In the space of people who have remembered who we are, why we are here, and who lives within us, it's only a matter of time before the cruelties of the world begin at last to recede from our midst.

May God's peace
extend through me.

I do not seek peace for myself alone, for I am not alone in the universe. May God's mantle of peace be placed upon me, and extend through me to bless the world.

God's greatest gift to me is a calm in my heart. Within that calm, may I find my wisdom. Through my wisdom, may I find my strength. And seeing my strength, may others find a strength within themselves.

God's gifts are never meant for any of us alone, for we are blessed and healed together. I receive God's gifts today on behalf of everyone. May my life be a channel through which they emerge into the world.

Aware of my weaknesses, I surrender them to God.

Instead of trying to hide my faults, I consciously aim to find them in order to deliver them to God. What I give to Him, He will take from me. He will not punish me but correct me. I do not fear God's vengeance, for God is never vengeful.

My greatest gift to Him and others is to be who I am capable of being. May today be a day of growth for me. May I not repeat old patterns, but break through into the regions of my highest self. May God take away from me all that is false, and fortify in me His beauty and His truth.

Dear God,

I seek to be
Who I am capable of being.
Take away from me
The things I think
That hide Your light in me.
May today be a day
When I break free
Of old habits of fear
That bind me.

Amen.

I increase my faith in miracles today.

Looking around me, there are reasons to believe in the power of my problems and the problems of the world. But I place my faith in miracles instead. There is no problem that love will not solve; my knowing this, attesting to this, and practicing this makes me a miracle-worker.

Thinking of one thing that seems to be an intractable problem, and I place the light of God around it. I use my mind to affirm that in Him all things are possible. I leave no room in my mind for doubt that this is so. With this refusal, I increase the possibility that a miracle will occur.

May I not be tempted to believe the testimony of my senses before the testimony of God. In any situation, may I remember the possibility of infinite possibility. May my mind thus be a conduit of miracles, as I have faith that they exist in God in unlimited supply.

I use the power of a positive attitude to uplift any situation.

My doubt, fear, negativity, and judgment have destructive power. My faith, love, positivity, and blessing have miraculous power. I will use my power wisely today.

Sometimes it's just an encouraging word, a tender touch, or a friendly smile that can bring hope to someone's heart. Such moments represent God's love on earth. I will be His representative today, as I try my best to bring love and hope to any circumstance.

Wherever I go, may there be more love and peace because I'm there. May my mind be ever alert to ways I can ease the path for someone. Dear God, please save me from a life lived only for myself.

REFLECTION

On Burning Through Pain

Chaos often fosters the greatest creativity. Breakdowns often precede the greatest breakthroughs. And when the pain is greatest is often when we're on the brink of the greatest realization.

The ego would prefer that we not look directly into the darkness. It would not have us *investigate* our pain, for that is when we can learn from it. The ego knows that crisis often leads to that pivotal moment when we fall to our knees and ask God for help. The ego is endangered by crisis, preferring that a mild river of misery simply run through the background of our lives, never bad enough to make us question where it comes from or what it means. Yet that painful moment, endured and transformed, is our chance to "rout Satan and remove him forever." When the pain is burned through rather than numbed, when our darkness is brought to light and then forgiven, then and only then can we move on. And move on we do. The ego knows this, and stakes its life on the fact that we don't.

What I give to others
I will receive.

What I put into the universe, the universe will put to me. I cannot escape the law of Cause and Effect, which is my protection when I am loving and my teacher when I am not. Today I choose to be generous, for generosity is in my self-interest. What I give to others I receive.

I will not be tempted today to deny, however subtly, the ways I withhold love from others. I will not feign confusion about the genesis of unfortunate events in my life, when I know in my heart what I did or did not do to cause them. I atone for my errors and begin again today, knowing love and love alone will guide me truly.

I seek to give today what I wish to receive. May I give love, understanding, forgiveness, and encouragement. May I listen well, nurture well, and speak with kindness. And when I deviate, may I be forgiven.

May I remember that every heart is fragile.

I am always so sensitive to my own fragile heart, while for-getting that others are as fragile as I am. All of us fear at times, and all of us love. All of us struggle, and all of us yearn. All of us hurt at times, and all of us at times hurt others.

May I be less sensitive to my every emotional cut and bruise, and more sensitive to the pain of others. May the scope of my compassion extend far beyond myself, and include a deeper consideration for hidden suffering in everyone. The scars of the heart might be hidden from view, but all of us carry them and all of us desire love.

Dear God,

Please heal my selfish heart
And make me more sensitive
To the pain of others.
May I feel compassion
For all suffering,
Not just my own.
May Your heart beat
Through mine.
And so it is.

Amen.

God is my source.

Whether I had the most wonderful parents, abusive ones, or even none at all, God is my ultimate mother and father. He is my source and my continual nurturer. My spiritual self is parented by God.

I receive the heavenly inheritance of the mind that God bequeaths to me. I am entitled as His child to the miracles that follow, whenever I remember whose child I am. May I think and act as befits my true origin.

I receive God's parenthood and my identity as His child. I detach from the false conditioning of the world, receiving the love that is my past, my present, and my future. I rejoice in that which is my true origin and my true life. Amen.

When justice calls to me, may I always respond.

Though I live a life of plenty, there are those in the world who suffer unjustly. They are bowed down in sorrow and suffering by systems over which they have no control. May my life, in whatever way possible, help ease the burden of those who suffer from the injustices of the world.

May I not forget that I am here to extend the compassion of God, to help repair the world, to heal the heart of humanity. Whatever I can do, with my love and with my efforts, may spirit guide me and give me the power to do.

Dear God,

May love pour down upon me
And use me as its vehicle.
May my life in some way be of service
To those who suffer.
May my efforts in some way bring justice
To those in need of it.
May my life in all ways be
Yours.

Amen.

REFLECTION

On Knowing That What
We Want Already Exists

The Bible's adage "Blessed are those who have faith and cannot see" means "Empowered are those who remember there is a truer truth, even when circumstances tempt them to believe otherwise."

When a pilot cannot see the horizon because of low visibility he or she doesn't assume that the horizon has disappeared. At a time of low visibility, the pilot flies on instruments that can gauge the situation more clearly than he or she can. Faith is like flying on instruments: it's acting on the assumption that just because you can't see a possibility at the moment doesn't mean that it's not there.

It's easy enough to have faith in God's infinite abundance when we have millions of dollars sitting in the bank; it's easy enough to have faith in love when we're receiving a lot of it; and it's easy enough to have faith in the power of peace when there is no war. But when it's hard to have faith is when we need it the most. By faith, we bring forth what we want, by knowing that it already exists in a realm we cannot yet see.

My body is a temple to the spirit of God.

My body is but a learning device, not my eternal home. I surrender it to God to use for His purposes. May my body be a shining example of how the things of the world, when reflecting holiness, take on the radiance of the spirit.

May my hands and feet, what I say, and what I do, all glorify the higher purposes of God. May His guidance within my mind determine the doings of my body. May my body be a temple to the emanations of my soul.

Dear God,

I surrender to You my body.
Please use it for Your purposes
And free it from the clutches
Of fear.
May love determine
Both its function and its activity.
May I live in my body
In health and joy.

Amen.

May war be no more.

In a world where every child is born of God's love, where every heart yearns to connect, and every mother prays that her child be protected, still yet we wage war. God forgive us.

In a world where every heart yearns for peace and every nation needs a rest from violence, where everyone prays that war not come near them if it need come at all, still yet we wage war. God forgive us. Show us another way.

Dear God,

Please forgive humanity
For the heinous thoughts
And cold, cruel actions
That occur on this blessed earth.
May thoughts of peace
And yearnings for love
Swell up as though a mighty wave.
May the world be washed clean
Of the wicked thoughts
Of fear and separation
That tear at our souls
And destroy our bodies.
May war be no more.

Amen.

Death is but a veil,
not an end.

While the body dies, the spirit does not. Let me not forget that those whom I have loved but lost to death are not lost at all. Rather, they dwell in the placid realm beyond time and space. They are not lost to me and I am not lost to them.

May a golden cord entwine my heart to those I love who have passed beyond the veil. May my inner eye be opened, that I might see the reality of eternal life. May death not tempt me to forget that what and whom God creates is created forever.

Dear God,

I place in Your hands my sorrow
And grief
Over anyone's death.
May my mind be healed of the delusions of the world,
That I might truly see
That life goes on forever.
May my heart be opened
To the higher truth
Of life unending.
And so it is.

Amen.

I accept the reality of what is, even when the moment is painful.

Tears can come bearing important gifts. Often it is our saddest moments that lead to our greatest growth. One of the most powerful lines in the Bible is one of its simplest: "Jesus wept."

My task is not to avoid painful emotion, but rather to transform it at its roots. I cannot do this if I don't move through my emotions authentically, truly asking myself what lessons they hold for me. If I would transcend my sadness, I must experience it first; I am ready to do both.

Today I allow myself permission to truly feel what is in my heart, both the happiness and the sadness there. I don't resist the emotional waves that rise up in me, but rather witness and accept them and surrender them to God. That way they are alchemized and turned into the bridge to my deliverance. Amen.

REFLECTION

On Having Faith in Miracles

L ove's miracles are being created in every given moment, unobstructed by anything carried over from the past. *That is the way the universe operates.* Faith in love doesn't determine love's power, but it does determine whether or not we *experience its power.*

You can misuse the power of your mind, but you can't eradicate the power of your mind. You can put your hands in front of your eyes and complain the room is dark, but you can't turn off the eternal light of God. The universe is infinitely and eternally lit with the light of new possibility, whether we're willing to consider it fact or not. We can have faith and have miracles, or we can deny faith and deflect them. The choice is huge but it is clear.

The present moment holds the key to my deliverance.

How often we move too quickly through life, running from moment to moment as if afraid of too deep an experience of any single instant. Yet what is my fear of the present? Why do I feel I must escape it and move on to the future when the present is where my treasure lies?

If I seek to escape the present moment, I will never escape the problems of the past. It is the present that holds the key to my deliverance, as I allow myself to dwell fully within it, embrace its meaning, and respond to it from my heart.

I give the present to God that I might dwell within it with greater understanding. I stop seeking to get somewhere, and embrace that in any moment I already am somewhere. I allow the glory of the present moment to bring to me its gifts. I receive them with all my heart.

I put all fear of lack into
the hands of God.

Today I remember that we live in an abundant universe, in which any worldly lack is automatically compensated for by spirit. Wherever I or others have diminished my worldly good, the universe has an automatic plan for my increase. Today I will not be tempted to forget this.

It is my faith and patience, not anxiety or impulsive action, that will return to me my good. The key to my external abundance is the abundance of love in my heart.

Dear God,

I surrender to You
The fear in my heart,
That there is not enough,
That I will not be taken care of,
That all things will go wrong.
Transform my thinking
That I might see that in You
There is only perfection and abundance
And I am at home in You.

Amen.

Relationships are lessons in my soul growth.

Relationships are spiritual assignments, people being brought together who represent maximal potential for each person's soul growth. I can walk away from my assignments, but I cannot walk away from the lessons they present to me.

I will learn the lesson of each relationship, or the lesson will reappear in my life until I do. My ego focuses on the faults of others, but my spirit focuses on me. Where was I in ego, living from the past, blaming rather than blessing? Where do I need to lighten up, get over myself, get off my high horse? Where do I need to forgive or ask forgiveness? Where do I need to atone or make amends? Am I releasing someone else to their highest good and wishing them only peace?

Dear God,

I place my relationship with _____
In Your hands.
Please lift our bond
Above the conflicts and illusions of the world.
May I see only the innocence in them
And they see only the innocence in me.
May forgiveness wash us clean.

Amen.

Negative emotions need to be released, not suppressed.

Having negative emotions doesn't make me a bad person; it means only that I'm in need of healing. Healing is a detox process, in which things come up in order to be released. God can only take from us what we are willing to give to Him, and how can I give to Him what I myself have not first looked at?

Feelings need to be accepted as they are before they can transform. As I release my negative feelings in an appropriate context—neither projecting them onto another person, nor condemning myself for having them—I begin the inner work necessary to change them. I accept that they are there, release them to God, and pray that He will change my mind about whatever situation has caused them. Thus my miracle begins.

Dear God,

I give to You, not hide from You,
My negative feelings
About anyone or anything.
I know you do not judge me,
But rather You will deliver me
From the insanity in my mind.

Amen.

REFLECTION

On Living in an Enchanted World

When you remember that you're a spiritual being, that God alone is the source of your power, and that the universe is inherently designed to provide for your needs, then you are thinking in a miracle-minded way. You are exercising dominion over the mortal plane by remembering you are not *of* it. You will find yourself living in an enchanted universe. You'll *just happen* to be seated next to someone on an airplane who is destined to be your new best friend. You'll *just happen* to think up some fabulous new project and attain effortless success in some non-traditional way. You'll *just happen* to meet someone in line at Starbucks who makes a casual comment that completely rocks your world.

Why? Because there is a realm of infinite creativity that exists *beyond* the mortal mind yet *within* the Mind of God. This is not fantasy, but rather the spiritual reality of the universe. If you choose not to believe this, that is your choice; if you choose to believe it, that is your miracle.

Character defects are not where we're bad but where we're wounded.

Character defects are not where we're bad but where we're wounded. That does not mean we're not responsible for them, but only that admitting them should not bring shame. We were born to become more perfect expressions of God, and facing our imperfections is part of the process involved in getting there.

Often our character defects have their genesis in childhood wounds, but it doesn't really matter where we got them—they're ours now. As we admit them and release them, we start the process of their dissolution.

There is nothing God cannot do, including lifting me up from the depths of my despair. Whatever pain I might feel, He both sees it and understands it. As long as I will show Him my wound—no matter how ugly the face it takes in me—He will heal it, for such is His love.

I honor a balance of masculine and feminine, in myself and in the world.

I seek to be in my life both assertive and passive, both driven to achieve as well as relaxed in the arms of God. May I receive from the divine and then give to the world, in an endless cycle of yin and yang energies that make me both strong and pliable.

I honor in myself and in others both the healthy masculine as well as the healthy feminine, knowing that both are necessary to create a beautiful world. I seek to serve the calling of both, as I encounter them and they move through me.

May our world be healed of the imbalance of masculine and feminine. May I serve the rebalancing by which feminine forces of nurturing and love will again hold sway, as they must if we are to survive. Amen.

I have infinite potential for greatness.

All of us carry within us an infinite potential for greatness. Even the geniuses among us have but scratched the surface of what all of us are programmed to achieve, once we manifest our full divine light. I, like all of humanity, have only just begun to spread my wings.

I willingly detach myself from the prejudices and judgments of the world, that I might be lifted above the downward pull of fear-based thought. I dedicate my life to the evolutionary lure of a higher state of awareness, not only in what I think but also in what I do. Thus shall I grow more fully today into the manifestation of my God-given potential.

I will not succumb to limited thoughts about myself today. I know that through God, who lives with me, I am always on my way to something greater than I have known before. The universe is a universe of constant increase, and I am a child of the universe.

I consciously participate in the world's transformation.

Inertia means the tendency of the object to move in whatever direction it's been moving, until there is the introduction of a counterforce. Today I consciously and proactively participate in a counterforce to the world's despair: a field of peace and love.

When enough of us love, fear will dissolve. When enough of us find peace in our hearts, war will cease. When enough of us stand on what we know to be true, falsehoods will no longer hold sway. May my thoughts and actions today help get us to "enough of us." May my entire being read, "I'm in."

I choose to be awake, though many slumber. I choose to stand on the truth of love, though many are lost in fear. I choose to be part of the solution, though many are at the effect of the problem. I choose to be a vessel of courage, though accommodation be the order of the day.

REFLECTION

On How Blessed You Are

Nothing about your material circumstances has the power to stop the engine of cosmic intention that you be blessed. And you are blessed "eternally," which means moment after moment after moment. In any instant, regardless of what has happened in the past, the universe has arranged and is continuing to arrange infinite possibilities for you to prosper.

It might offend your sense of "realism" to believe this. Surely, things can't be that good. And yet, they are. The universe is programmed to manifest, through you, the highest possibilities for your creativity and joy. And that will never, ever change. God is intent on your deliverance from all forms of bondage to the freedom of unlimited love.

I will not accommodate myself to the dictates of fear. I commit myself to the ways of love.

Sometimes it seems easier to accommodate ourselves to the ways of an insane world than to stand up and say, "No." Sometimes it seems easier to just go along, to abide mediocrity, to not have to take the heat of a fearful world's approbation when we insist on doing what we feel is right.

Today I refuse to accommodate myself to the dictates of fear. I am part of the revolution of love now sweeping the world, saying "No" to fear and "Yes" to love. In whatever way I can, I contribute consciously to the emergence of a better world.

Though the world is weary and tired of the fight, I refuse to succumb to the slumber of fear. This is not the time to be numb, to acquiesce, to just go along. I will not accommodate myself to the ways of fear. I commit myself to the ways of love.

I include everyone today in the circle of my love.

My ego will always tell me that *other people are the problem.* It tempts me to blame, to judge, and to withhold forgiveness. Yet I realize that its main target is me. It would encase me in a shroud of fear.

Today I refuse to blame anyone. No matter what judgment arises in my mind, I ask spirit to reveal to me another interpretation of events. For what is not love is a call for love, and today I choose to see that in everyone. Thus shall I forge the miracle-worker's insight, and a miracle-worker's power. Amen.

My attack thoughts about anyone are attacks upon myself. My forgiveness of anyone is forgiveness of myself. Today I choose to see innocence beyond guilt, and calls for love behind all shrieks of fear. May I include everyone today in the circle of my love.

I surrender to a power
greater than my own.

In surrendering to God, I surrender to something bigger than myself—to a universe that knows what it's doing. When I stop trying to control events, they fall into a natural order, an order that works. I'm at rest while a power much greater than my own takes over, and it does a much better job than I could have done.

I can learn to trust that the power that holds galaxies together can handle the circumstances of my relatively little life. I choose to remember in any moment that a surrendered life is a more successful life, because it is under the control of a power much greater than my own.

Dear God,

I surrender to You
All I am and all I have.
Every thought, every feeling, every yearning,
I surrender to You.
I take my hands off the steering wheel.
Dear God, please drive.

Amen.

Love is the only
unalterable truth.

The mortal realm can be a place full of wonder and excitement, but it is not—even in its most intense manifestations—the world of ultimate truth. Only the reality of a radical, fundamental love is unalterable and eternal.

In the end, there is only love. This is the truth I will remember at the end of my life, or perhaps at the end of the life of a loved one. It's the truth I see when the superficial preoccupations that compete for my attention and rob me of my life force begin, at last, to melt away. Today, I accept the fundamental truth of my existence: that only love is real.

Love is the only ultimate; all else is a hallucination of the mortal mind. As I see this, I penetrate the veil of illusion that blinds me to my power and my good.

REFLECTION

On Love as Strength and Not Weakness

Making love the bottom line doesn't make you a doormat. It doesn't mean you're compelled to do anything anyone ever asks of you. Love always gives the loving response—but sometimes the loving response is "no."

Love is not weakness, but strength. It gives us clarity, wisdom, and astuteness about people. It gives us intuitive gifts that help us discern situations we might not otherwise understand. We never need fear that in seeking God's guidance in something, we will be led to sacrifice our own good. Sacrifice is the life we live *before* we dedicate ourselves to God. God is not the way to sacrifice; He is the end to sacrifice. That is how loved we are.

I surrender
my critical nature.

Everything we do is infused with the energy with which we do it.

Even if I think I'm giving constructive criticism, if I say something in an effort to change someone, then they will feel repelled. What I might think is a sharing will come across as an attack. I pray today for the ability to communicate effectively, but with love.

Behavioral change is not enough to transform our communication skills. I cannot cover an attack with sugary icing, a sweet tone of voice, or therapeutic jargon and expect a miracle. For that, I need an authentic switch from fear to love. I pray today for the ability to honor the spiritual perfection in everyone, that they might feel my love no matter what I say.

Dear God,

Please redeem my personality,
That any sharp edges within me
Shall turn tender.
With every word I say,
May I heal and not harm.
And so it is.

Amen.

Today I am committed to forgiving someone I find hard to forgive.

Wherever I withhold love, I block my own good. Wherever I stay stuck in the past, I keep the present from unfolding miraculously. Wherever I see myself as having been victimized, I tie myself to the experience of victimization.

The part of me that can be offended, or victimized in any way, is not the real me. The real me lives in triumph and spiritual victory regardless of what I have been through or what has been done to me. Only my holding on to grievances can keep the universe from providing me with the miracle of a new beginning.

Dear God,

I surrender to You my grievances,
The people I cannot forgive,
The place where I hold on and cannot let go,
The darkness in my own heart.
Please remove the sickness
Of unforgiveness
From my soul.
And so it is.

Amen.

My body ages but
my spirit does not.

My body is merely a suit of clothes, a temporary container for my eternal spirit. As I identify more with my spirit, realizing that my essence is ageless, my thoughts about age will change. Accordingly, so will my body.

I am not burdened today by false beliefs about the vulnerability of my body to age or disease. I see the white light of spirit that races through every cell of my being, filling my body as well as my mind with the revitalizing power of love.

My body is a vessel through which my spirit can operate while in this world, and I am grateful for it. I wish to treat it with profound respect, yet not be tempted to see it as who I am. I am not my body, and my body is not me. My body is temporary and I am not.

Endless creativity is the natural state of my being.

God is in a continuous state of creativity, flowing within and through me every moment. With each thought I think, I open to receive the imprint of divinity upon my consciousness. I bask in the light that is Him within me.

All darkness of thought or feeling, all neurotic or fear-based patterns, and all despair or limitation dissolve as I drink in the powerful vibrations of love. They are replaced by the artistry of the divine, forming patterns of thought and behavior moving through me to create the beautiful, holy, and true.

God is the artist of the universe, the Creator of all things, and the designer of all life. I open my heart and mind, that I might be the paintbrush with which He paints and the vessel through which He pours forth His endless creativity and love.

REFLECTION

On What's Possible for You Now

On the mortal plane, none of us are perfect all the time. But on the spiritual plane, all of us are perfect all the time. Who we *really* are—perfect creations of God, unchangeable and unlimited, none of us more or less brilliant than anyone else—is the most positive self-concept possible. To identify yourself according to your spiritual rather than material reality is enlightenment. From this perspective, you see that you *are* the light. No thought or condition of darkness—that is, lack of love in your own mind or in anyone else's—has any bearing whatsoever on the truth of who you are or what the universe has planned for you. Your past, your mistakes, other people's opinions about you, even your failures do not in any way limit who you are or what is possible for you now.

Today I extend
compassion to myself.

The roughness of the world is hard on the heart; mine has been tested, as has everyone's. Today I acknowledge any bruises on my soul and deliver them to God. I know that in His hands they will be healed.

I own my pain, that I might heal whatever darkness it has spawned in me. I pray that neither others nor I will be affected by my mistakes. May my own compassion for what I have suffered help heal me where I hurt.

Dear God,

I surrender to You
The scars upon my heart,
The memories that sear,
And the sorrows that remain.
Please place Your hand upon me
And miraculously heal me,
That I might rise from the ashes
Of my past
And experience new life.

Amen.

All my talents
are of use to God.

Whatever talents I have, however seemingly insignificant, can be of use to God. Even if I think I have none, if I offer my life to Him, then new talents will emerge. Today I share my gifts with others as a way of sharing them with God.

I realize no gift is too large or too small to be used for divine purposes, to bring joy to someone, to help bring healing somewhere. I do not underestimate the magnitude of my gifts today. Through God, their potential for good is infinite.

I am not ashamed of my gifts today, however meager they may appear. For that which is surrendered to God is lifted to its highest creative potential, miraculously transforming from what might seem to be a tiny gift to become a mighty force.

No limits of the world
can limit me.

Nothing in my worldly circumstances defines me or limits me. As my mind is lifted above the fear of the world, I am delivered to the field of miraculous possibilities. I am fully loved, fully blessed, and fully of use to God at all times.

While the world might see my life as less than, no child of God is less than glorious. My spirit is abundant, though my worldly cup might be empty. And my mind is radiant, though the thinking of the world might confound me. Today I accept that I am a child of a boundless universe.

Dear God,

Remove the chains that bind me,
In my mind and in my life.
Free me of any false beliefs
That limit my ability
To see.
Open my eyes
To my freedom
In You.

Amen.

I bless the abundance of others, in order to increase my own.

The ego's world is limited, but God's is not. On the material plane, there are only so many pieces of pie. But on the spiritual plane, there are an infinite number. My having a piece doesn't mean there is less for others, and others having a piece doesn't mean there is less for me.

There is enough for everyone. There is enough room for everyone to be beautiful. There is enough room for everyone to be successful. There is enough room for everyone to be loved. I generously wish for others what I most wish for myself, for what I bless in their lives I will allow into my own.

I will not jealously constrict my heart today, seeking to keep from others what I would keep to myself. For only what I give away do I keep, and what I seek to guard as my own I will lose. Such reversal of material law is the truth of the spiritual universe.

REFLECTION

On Moving Beyond Competition

E ach of us has a unique part to play in the healing of the world. Each of us is assigned by God a function that only we can fill. At the level of the divine, none of us are in competition with each other. We do not have to compete for a piece of the cosmic pie, for the universe has an infinite number of pieces of pie. Mine doesn't take away from yours, and yours doesn't take away from mine. There is more than enough space in the ultimate universe for all of us to prosper.

Just as the cells of the body are programmed each to do what they are supposed to do, collaborating with other cells to foster the health of the organ of which they are part, so each of us is divinely programmed to do what is best for us to do to contribute our greatest gifts to the world. As we celebrate other people's gifts, we increase the value of our own. Whatever we approve of in another's life, we allow ourselves to have. Whatever applause we give another, we are attracting to ourselves.

Love is not my weakness, but my strength.

Sometimes I feel that if I'm loving, vulnerable, and energetically unguarded, others will take advantage of me. In fact, it's my love and defenselessness that provide me with divine protection. My love attracts my greater good.

Love gives me strength. It guides me to clearer thinking, more meaningful reflections, a kinder way of being, and a more attractive personality. It opens me to a creative flow. It is the key to my success in life, and the source of my inspiration.

Love is the power of God flowing through me. It is my privilege in life to channel His power for the good of the entire world. With every thought I think, I have the opportunity to extend the force that blesses all things. I am grateful and humbled before His power within me.

DAY 297

May my words emerge from the silence of my soul.

I f I speak with my mouth, others will hear me with their ears. But only if I speak from my heart will others hear me with their hearts. Today may my words emerge from somewhere deeper than my intellect—and never from anger or defensiveness. May my words emerge from the silence of my soul.

Words have power to heal or to harm; I dedicate mine to the healing power of love. May I become a healer of the spoken word.

Dear God,

May Your spirit
Be upon me when I speak,
Infusing my words with
The energy of love.
May my words convey Your power
And Yours alone.

Amen.

I step back and
let God lead the way.

I stand humbly before a power that is in me but not of me. I am not the divine source, but merely a faucet through which its waters flow into the world. I find power as a human being as I defer to the power of the spirit.

Placing myself in service to God, I pray that His love move through me to bless the world. I take a step back today with my personality, that I might more clearly reflect His gentleness and love. As I step back, He leads the way for me to follow.

Meekness and mildness carry invisible power. The meek shall inherit the earth because of their strength, having stepped back and allowed a greater power to flow through them. Today I choose to step back with the force of my personality, that I might step forward with the force of my spirit.

I greet everyone I meet today
with the love that's in my heart.

Today I will not be tempted by the thinking of the world.
May I remember that everyone I see, or meet, or even
think of is an innocent child of God. Silently and invisibly, I
greet them with love.

Though my ego might tell me otherwise, I will remember
that my only purpose is to love and forgive. There, within that
space of consciousness, I will find my power as well as my joy
in living. May neither fear nor judgment divert me from my
chosen path.

Dear God,

Post angels around my mind today,
To remind me of love
And protect me from fear.
May Your light surround each person I see
And show itself to me.

Amen.

REFLECTION

On Not Turning Away from Love

Love makes us wake up in the morning with a sense of purpose and a flow of creative ideas. Love floods our nervous system with positive energy, making us far more attractive to prospective friends and associates. Love fills us with a powerful charisma, enabling us to produce new ideas and projects, even within circumstances that seem to be limited. Love leads us to atone for our errors and clean up the mess when we've made mistakes. Love leads us to act with impeccability, integrity, and excellence. Love leads us to serve, to forgive, and to hope.

So why would we turn away from love? What is the subconscious resistance to such a powerful force for good? Why do we fear the very thing that makes our lives worthwhile? Just asking the question takes us closer to the answer: that that which leads us away from love is never our friend, never true self-care, and never from God. The ego is our own self-hatred merely posing as our friend. Once we know that, the false friend begins to lose its power to lure us away from love.

Every situation is planned as a chance for me to grow.

Today I will recognize everything that happens as an opportunity to grow—a chance to embody who I am capable of being. If I am tempted to weakness, I will choose to be strong. If I am tempted to anger, I will choose to forgive. And if I am tempted by fear, I will choose to love.

I know the universe is set up to support me in becoming my fully actualized self. Whether the lesson is easy or the lesson is challenging, I will see each moment as my chance to grow. This way I will learn what love is, and I will learn who I am.

Dear God,

No matter who I meet today
And no matter what occurs,
Help me to remember love.
Guide my mind
And open my heart.
May I see Your love in everything,
That I might know the truth.

Amen.

I surrender my destiny
to a loving God.

I cannot know what will happen tomorrow, or what would be best to occur in my life. I will not try to control my destiny. I surrender my future into the hands of God.

I need not struggle to make things happen, and I need not plan how my life will unfold. I need only respond to the invitation of each moment, to show up fully in excellence and love. Thus shall I be guided by life itself, and delivered to my greater good.

Today I surrender to the flow of love, knowing it is a river that leads me to a peaceful place. I give all goals, all plans, and all attachments to God. What He wills is my highest good; in my life and in the world, may His will be done.

Today I pray for those who do not love me.

Perhaps there is someone who does not understand me, who does not accept me, and does not love me. Let me not respond to their judgment with judgment. Today I respond to their judgment with love.

Whatever has so locked their hearts that they cannot see into mine, may God free them. Whatever has wounded their souls that they cannot appreciate that I have wounds as well, may God heal them. Whatever fear so blinds them to love, may love yet be shown to them.

Dear God,

Today I pray for someone
Who withholds their approval, their support, or their love
From me.
Send a miracle into my heart.
May I rise above reaction or blame.
Free both of us to the love
Of each other
That lies beyond this veil.

Amen.

I surrender my jealousy and
pray it be transformed.

If I am jealous, I withhold my blessing from those who have what I wish to have. Yet jealousy itself will block my reception. Only what I bless in others do I then attract toward myself.

In the material world, supply is limited; while in the spiritual world, supply is unlimited. No one else's good diminishes my own. May I celebrate abundance wherever I see it and thus attract it into my life.

Let me not be waylaid by petty thoughts and ungenerous feelings. May I not think that someone else shouldn't have what I know in my heart that I want. Today I bless those who have what I would wish to have, and release all jealous thoughts to God.

REFLECTION

On Knowing It Now

You are a child of God, carrying the eternal mark of your perfect source. You are naturally entitled to miracles because love is what you are. This is not an arrogant appraisal of the ego, but rather a humble acceptance of God's truth. You just happen to have within you the eternal light of the universe.

Your parents might not have told you that. Your teachers might not have told you that. Your friends might not have told you that. But all of that is irrelevant. If you've lived twenty or seventy years not knowing until now that you're the light of all creation, the important thing is that you know it now.

Giving to others is an act of self-love.

Only what I give do I get to keep, and what I withhold shall be taken from me. Withholding my love is an act of self-betrayal, and giving to others is an act of self-love.

Today I will not be focused solely on myself, for my salvation lies in loving others. May I not obsess about my own concerns, when the concerns of so many others are greater. May I not be tempted to deny my good by denying it to others.

It is neither co-dependent nor sacrificial to love others as I love myself. Rather, it is the hallmark of enlightenment. Today I seek to love more deeply than I have loved before, that I might know the joy of using my mind for the purpose it was created to serve.

Today I receive all the love that is given me.

How often do I not truly take in the love that is shown me. I don't linger long enough on a loving letter, breathe in deeply enough the acknowledgment of a friend, or allow myself to value enough the hug of a little child.

I complain about a lack of love, yet often I deflect the love that is shown me. Today I will receive more fully the love that is there, no longer demanding that it come in a form I think I would prefer. Today I am grateful for the love I receive.

How often I've pushed love away by not recognizing it was there. How often I've been ungrateful for love, and then watched as it dissolved. May such patterns end in me today, as I resolve to be watchful for the love all around me.

Today I am more alert to the needs of others.

How self-sabotaging is my selfishness, when I look but do not see the suffering of others. Too seldom do I notice the courage of those who wake up each day and do their best with painful circumstances. Today I will be more alert to the suffering of others.

It is hard to face in ourselves the trait of self-centeredness. But in facing it we are saved from it. The only way to truly love ourselves is to open our hearts to each other.

Generosity toward others is an act of self-interest, for in loving others I attract more love. May no one's suffering be meaningless to me, that I might know the meaning of life. Free me from a selfish heart. Amen.

The universe sees everything.
The universe sees me.

There is nothing in the universe unseen by the divine. God knows each thought I think and each action I take, and I will see the effects of both. May I cause only good, that I receive only good.

May I not be tempted to think I am ever "unseen," for God's eyes see through to my heart. He rewards me for my love, yet He does not judge me for my lack of it. My love He will increase; and my lack of love—should I admit it and surrender it for healing—will be the stuff of His next miracle. Such is the awesomeness of God.

Dear God,

I know You see me,
Both when I stand tall and when I stumble.
I know You smile when I love the world,
And cry for me when I do not.
I give to You my broken places,
The wounds that keep me from opening my heart,
And know I shall be healed.

Amen.

REFLECTION

On Moving Mountains

We've all got the "right stuff" because all of us are hosts to God; His voice, and not the fear-based ego's, is the voice we can listen to and learn to follow. Each of us is meant to channel the spiritual forces of talent, creativity, and intelligence. This is nothing to take personal credit for, but nothing to apologize for either. As a child of God, you *just happen* to be the recipient of endless power and possibility. Whether or not you've always known this, or practiced it, there lies within you in this very moment the latent ability to create and achieve beyond your wildest dreams.

And this never changes. No mortal condition diminishes the power of God. It doesn't matter what your résumé is, or how many degrees you have. It doesn't matter what mistakes you've made, or how the economy is doing. It matters only where you place your consciousness now. Know who you are and who lives within you, and moving mountains will seem small compared to what you can do.

I take full responsibility
for the state of my life.

I take full responsibility for the state of my life. As I change my mind from fear to love, all situations miraculously heal. I am not a victim of the world I see.

I do not abdicate the power of my mind. I empower myself by surrendering to God. I surrender all of my thoughts to Him, and pray that I be lifted to the holy mind-set whereby I myself am a creator of good.

The price I pay for not taking full responsibility for my life is an inability to change it. God Himself resides in my mind, empowering me to change any circumstance by remembering to love. Today I will use the power I am given, to heal my life by loving the people who are in it.

I would be free of the burden of self.

I will not take myself too seriously today. As I lighten up, I will see the light. Too much focus on myself only blinds me to the truth.

As I free myself of the burden of self, the chains that bind me shall fall away. Emptying myself, I shall be filled with God. Exalting God, I shall be exalted. Losing myself, I shall find myself in Him.

Dear God,

Please take from me
Any false impressions of who I am.
Release me from chains that bind me
To a limited perception of others and myself.
Free me to see the unlimited life
That is You, that is me, that is everyone.

Amen.

The universe is my home.
I am safe here.

God sees me and cares for me, as He sees and cares for everyone. I belong in this world, and He abides here with me. The universe is my home, and I am safe here.

May I feel the arms of God around me. May I feel the warmth of the sun upon me. May I feel the angels surround and uplift me, as I go about my way.

So often I have walked the world in fear of what it will do to me, cowering before imagined demons, retreating from others and even from myself. May light dissolve all darkness in my mind today, and return me to my inner knowing that love is real and fear is not.

I needn't struggle
for what is mine.

I needn't apologize for the fact of my existence. Angels themselves celebrate it, for I am a creation of God. I am adored by Him, as is everyone. I need but to remember this, to experience what is mine.

I have a voice that is mine alone. I have talents that are mine alone. I have a function that is mine alone. Such are the gifts He has given me. I needn't struggle for what is mine.

Dear God,

May I not be tempted to believe
That I am less than You created me to be.
May false humility not deter me
From appreciation of Your power within me.
May true humility fill my mind and heart,
That I might know my strength.

Amen.

DAY 315

On Surrendering Our Anger

It doesn't matter if someone tells you that you "deserve" to be angry—you *deserve*, of course, to feel whatever you want to feel! But the only way to experience miracles is to think about situations in a miracle-minded way. Holding on to anger hurts no one but yourself. As it says in *A Course in Miracles,* "Do you prefer to be right or to be happy?"

The universe knows if you were hurt, and it is already on the case to make right whatever wrong occurred. Your anger, if it lingers, throws a wrench in the machine of the miraculous universe. Something miraculous happens when we say, "I am angry but I am willing not to be. Dear God, help me see this situation differently. Amen."

May the animals be blessed.

Today I remember the animals of the world, our cohabitants of this precious planet. I recognize their vulnerability, as well as the harm we sometimes do to them.

May careless, even cruel behavior toward animals be forever removed from the earth. May my heart be open to ways I can be of service to them. May the relationship between humans and animals be lifted to its highest place.

Dear God,

Please bless the animals.
Protect them
From the actions of those with cold hearts.
May we be proper stewards
Of these precious creations in our midst.

Amen.

I am here to soar with the wings God has given me.

Each of us has a unique function on the earth. I do not serve the world by withholding my gifts in the name of modesty. Remembering I am no more or less special than anyone else, I am free to soar with the wings God has given me.

Until I do, my place in the universe is left unfilled. My love, my abilities, my skills are mine alone, and I was born to extend them as a light unto darkened places. Today, in every moment, may I be the embodiment of the light of the world.

Dear God,

You have given me such special gifts,
And yet I block them when I deny Your love.
Today may I remember
The holy purpose You have given me,
That I might find my talents
And be blessed thereby.

Amen.

Today may I be a better mate/ friend/parent/employer/employee.

Whatever role I play in life, I am there to be more, and do more, than appears. While the ego focuses in any situation on my needs as I define them, my only true need is to be the most shining light I can be.

As I increase my own giving—a greater generosity, deeper understanding, and more loving attitude toward others—my life will be thereby blessed. May I participate today in all of my relationships from a more healed and holy place.

May I view each role I play as God intended it to be: the avenue through which miracles pour into me and through me. May I not limit my perceptions today to the drama of the mortal plane, but rather see every relationship as a holy one.

Today I seek to love everyone.

When I see anyone today, I will bless him or her silently. When I enter a room, I will send my love before me. In thinking of anyone, I will surrender the relationship to God.

Today I seek to love everyone. My mind and heart were created to be a vessel of God's compassion, and today I pray to be aligned with His intention for my life.

Dear God,

It isn't easy
To be a lover of the world,
But today I will try.
May my love expand to include everyone,
Both those I like
And those I do not like.
Help me love more deeply,
That my life might be of greatest use.

Amen.

REFLECTION

On Choosing to Be Better

Our clinging to old wounds might inspire sympathy for a time, or even temporary support. But it will not inspire invitations to start over, from other people or from the universe itself. Bitterness is hardly the personality trait that someone out there is looking to hire, partner with, promote, or invest in.

No matter what we have endured, there is probably someone out there who has been through worse. There are people who have experienced the most heinous things, and have found a path forward into happiness and peace. There are things that happen in life after which we know we will never be the same. But which way it goes—whether we become bitter or better—is a choice that only we can make.

Today I have the courage
to reach for my dreams.

I know in my heart that it isn't outer force, but merely lack of courage, that keeps me from living the life I desire. I recognize the fear that keeps me from reaching for my dreams.

The miracles I seek will not unfold unless I claim the love that casts out fear. Today I will not hide behind the excuses that I give myself; I will deepen my willingness to serve the light within me, wherever it leads and whatever it might ask of me.

Dear God,

I cower in fear at times
Before the calling of my soul,
The call to greatness,
The call to enlightenment,
The call to You.
Please help me make the choice for love,
That I might live the life
I truly desire
And manifest my dreams.

Amen.

I turn away from habits of weakness and cultivate habits of strength.

I know I have habits of weakness in certain areas of my life. Today, I remember that with the help of God I can change my mind and change my ways.

Who I have been, I need not be now. What I have done, I need not do now. How I have acted, I need not act now. I call upon the spirit of God to break the chains that bind me to the weakness of my former self. I choose strength, and know that God Himself supports my choice.

I know God Himself will help me be the person He would have me be. Today I eschew the habits of weakness that keep me bound in suffering. I claim the power of God within me to break all cords that bind me to the past and to deliver me to my better self. Amen.

I seek to be the best friend
I can be to those who
have befriended me.

How often I take for granted the love that is shown me by my friends. I'm reminded today that our mortal lives are not forever, and that our friendships on earth are but fleeting gifts.

May I remember to listen more, and say, "thank you" and "I love you" more to my friends. May I seek to understand what others are feeling, before telling them what I am feeling. May I be a less selfish friend, today and always.

Dear God,

I place in Your hands
My relationship with my friends.
May I be a better friend,
More supportive and understanding
And giving and compassionate.
Thus may my relationships
Fulfill their purpose
And make all of us whole.

Amen.

May I never be cynical.

It's easy to become pessimistic at times, to declare oneself too cool to care, too knowledgeable or reasonable to believe in miracles. Yet love is the power of God, and miracles occur naturally as expressions of love.

Today I will not allow cynicism to blind me to the infinite possibilities God provides. Miracles are all around me and I claim them as my own; may I see the light that is mine to see whenever I open my eyes.

May cynicism never close my eyes, nor pessimism poison my thinking. May I always be looking for the ray of light eternally on God's horizon. May my mind thus be a conduit for miracles and love.

REFLECTION

On the Atonement

When we take full responsibility for the places where we know in our hearts we underperformed in the past, or acted without integrity, or failed to respect opportunities and abundance that once were ours, we experience the miracle of the Atonement.

Atonement is a mental process through which we correct our perceptions, thus changing the trajectory of probabilities that unfold as a result. Atonement is like a spiritual reset button. It is a gift from God, providing us the opportunity to clear the karma of past mistakes by owning them, taking responsibility for them, admitting them, making amends for them, and doing whatever is possible to change the patterns of behavior that created the situations that now cause us shame.

We recognize past errors and pray, "I am willing to be different than I was before. Please show me how." The universe then corrects all limitations caused by our wrong-minded thinking. Guilt dissolves from our minds as thoughts of mercy and love replace it.

I see the world infused with light.

Regardless of the painful dramas of the world, I believe in a force more powerful than evil. I believe that in the presence of love, all fear will disappear. And I believe that people are essentially good.

I place myself in service to the mighty force of peace. I believe that there will yet be a turning of the human heart. I pray to be used in a great awakening that reminds us who we are, infusing our hearts and then our world with a light that casts out darkness and delivers us to love.

Dear God,

Bring forth the light of understanding
That enables us to see each other,
To love each other,
To forgive each other,
And thus to save the world.

Amen.

I will not judge whom
I know God loves.

God did not create the universe and then ask me to run it. He did not ask me to be judge and jury of anyone. He has only asked me to love.

How my ego would nail others to the cross of my own expectations! May I be delivered today to a more humble way of seeing, for only God can see into every heart. I will not judge whom I know He loves, and I know that He loves everyone.

May I be healed of my judgmental mind, which only serves to defeat me. As I judge I will surely be judged, for such is the law of perception. When my mind attacks anyone, my mind attacks me. May my mind become a vessel of love, and all judgment fall away.

I choose a more gentle perception
today of everyone and everything.

How harsh my mind can be, when I blame instead of
bless. I acknowledge the insanity of my thinking, when
I attack whom I know God loves.

May I be delivered to a new way of thinking. May gentleness and holiness come upon my heart today. May the spirit of
forgiveness renew my spirit and show me what love is.

Dear God,

Where I am harsh, please make me gentle.
Where I blame, please teach me to bless.
When I would close my heart,
Please keep it open.
Thus shall I be changed
In my spirit
And my life will be transformed.

Amen.

Forgiveness frees me to live a different kind of life.

The only way to be free of my past is if I'm willing to free others from theirs. May my focus be changed today— from what others have done to hurt me to what others have done to love me, and from what others have not given me to what I have not given them.

I extend my perceptions beyond the mistakes of the body to the innocence of spirit, and from the darkness of the world to the light within our hearts. I choose to forgive, that I might feel forgiven. Forgiveness shall then free me to live a different kind of life.

Dear God,

Please remove the scales
That would blind my eyes
To the light that is all around me.
Help me to see the innocence in everyone
And the love in every heart.
Help me no longer dwell in darkness,
But rather bathe in eternal light.

Amen.

REFLECTION

On Where to Put Our Talents

The way to abundance is to surrender our abilities and talents, asking that they be used by God to help heal the world. Too many people feel that they have talent but simply don't know where to put it. We're not raised in a society that asks, "What are your gifts, and how can they make the world a more beautiful place?" We're usually asked something more like this: "What will you do to make a living?" This knocks us out of our natural rhythm, because the soul simply doesn't think that way. There is no more natural proclivity than to serve love. Something very powerful happens when we pray, "Dear God, please use me." Making ourselves available to the universe for its loving purposes, we are taken up on our offer immediately.

My body is healthy and vital, washed in holy light.

As I go about my day today, I use my mind to heal and restore my body. I do not take in the stress of the world, for I relax in the arms of God. I continually pour white light into the cells of my physical self, that they might be fed by the divine.

My body is a learning device that supports me in my soul's journey. I do not abuse it or misuse it, for it is a holy temple. It contains my energy for the purposes of my life on earth. How holy is this gift that God has given me.

Dear God,

May my body be healthy and whole.
I surrender it to You
To be used for Your purposes—
To give and receive the gifts of love
In all I say and do.
May it contain Your light
And express Your vibrancy.
And so it is.

Amen.

Where I am broken, I am healing.
And one day I will be strong.

As I walk through the valleys of failure or loss, I shall not forget Who walks with me. Such times, though hard, are temporary. I feel my pain, but hold on to my faith.

Even now, in the midst of my tears, I know God is watching. He has posted angels around me, who will guide me to the other side of my pain. I will be shown what it is that I need to see, and one day I will laugh again. For my God is an awesome God.

Dear God,

Though I am weakened,
Please make me strong again.
Where I am damaged, please make me whole.
Though my heart is broken,
Please bring back my joy.

Amen.

I bless my loved ones who have passed beyond the veil.

Today I think thoughts of love toward those who touched my life while here on earth, and then continued on their journey. My family and my friends—my beloved companions—may they feel my love where they are now. And in my heart, may I feel theirs.

Death is but an illusion of the mortal mind, for truly life goes on forever. As the body drops, the spirit soars to new heights. Neither sickness nor death will tempt me to forget that in God there is life unending.

May God fill my heart with an inner knowing that those who have left have not left at all, for they remain in His heart and mine. I feel peace as I remember them, for I know they are not gone. May they, and I, rest peacefully in the arms of God.

I am open to change,
and do not resist it.

I will not resist what occurs today. I open my heart to new places, new people, and new chapters of my life. For I know that all is planned according to God's will that I be blessed.

I will not live in fear of the unfamiliar. I am open to the changes that are part of life, for they always bear new gifts. The past is over, but the present is filled with the infinite gifts of God.

I face today with a courageous heart. I ignore the voices that would hold me to my past, and dwell eagerly in the newness of now. I dwell in the present with an open heart, knowing my destiny will unfold with miracles and joy.

REFLECTION

On God's Plan

Trust that there is a perfect plan for the unfolding of your highest good, which your rational mind cannot formulate. God's plan works, and yours doesn't. You cannot know how your part fits best into a larger plan for the healing of the world, but God does. Your job is merely to open your mind and open your heart so that a higher consciousness can then flow through you.

I greet new people with a kind and friendly heart.

Every meeting is according to divine assignment. May I see no strangers, but only friends whom I haven't met yet. May everyone who comes into my presence feel a peaceful welcome from my heart to theirs.

May all my encounters be holy today as I open my heart to everyone. May I bless each person in a room before I even enter it, and everyone around me while I stand in their midst. Thus shall I experience the miracles brought to me when my heart is open to love.

Dear God,

Please post Your angels around me
To always remind me
Of the beauty of Your children.
May I never forget to bless them,
Regardless of who they are.
May anyone in my presence
Feel Your peace and love.

Amen.

Kindness is the greatest power, without which I am weak.

U nless I am kind I am not aligned with love, regardless of my intentions. Kindness is God's key that unlocks any door. With kindness I work miracles, for kindness is the mark of love.

How easy it is to forget how fragile people are, not only myself but everyone. Today may I be kind to whomever I meet, that they might feel the blessed touch of someone sensitive to their heart.

Dear God,

I know I'm on earth to be kind to others.
How easily I am swayed by the ego's insistence
That something else, anything else,
Is surely more important.
Today I take a stand against the ego's insistence
And pray for an angel of kindness
To touch my soul.
May this seed bear fruit, dear God,
And make me a kinder person.

Amen.

In any moment, in any circumstance, a miracle will occur if I align myself with love.

There is no order of difficulty in miracles. One is not harder or bigger than another. I am a child of God, and God works miracles naturally. Miracles are built into the fabric of the universe, and I am entitled to them because of who I am.

Remembering who I am, I will not struggle today about anything. I release all cares, all burdens, and all questions to God. I will not constrict my energy, but rather relax into His loving arms. From there, every circumstance in my life shall be miraculously lifted to divine right order.

The more burdens I carry, the more temptation I experience to tighten, to worry, to control, to constrict. Yet today I remember to do the opposite. I remember that miracles will occur in whatever situation I release to love. Today I release them all.

I allow each moment to be exactly as it is.

I realize that my only true problem is separating myself from God. Yet how difficult it feels at times to truly trust that He is there. Today I open my heart and relax my mind, in order to experience His presence in my life.

I allow every moment to be exactly as it is. As I relax instead of trying to control, I see how all things get lifted to divine right order. God is here and He is active in my life, in any moment that I surrender to Him. May every instant of my life be holy.

Dear God,

I seek to release control today,
Loosening my tight grip
And surrendering my life to You.
What I release from my hands, dear God,
Please take into Your hands.
Take all that I cannot control
And make it beautiful.

Amen.

REFLECTION

On Your Highest Function

On the spiritual plane, you have no competitors. There is no competition for your position, as you are a unique expression of the Mind of God. You not only have a place in the universe; you have an essential *function* in the universe. Only you can do the job of being you, and the universe itself is incomplete without you. It is not arrogant but humble to realize this, as you place yourself in service to the greatest drama there is: the actualization of your own potential.

Your highest function is simply to be the person you are capable of being, and from that effort—the development of your kindness and positivity, your vulnerability and availability to life, your calling will emerge.

May God's will be done.

How easily the deeper truths reveal themselves when we allow ourselves to see. May God's will (thought) be done (be manifest) on earth (in my experience) as it is in heaven (my abstract understanding). Forever and ever (moment after moment after moment). Amen (and so it is).

Today, I surrender all I think and all I do to the will of God, the thought of love. May the love I bring forth help cast out the fear of the world.

May my mind be a channel through which the thoughts of heaven make their way into the world. May God's emanations of love find expression through me in any way possible. May God's will be done in my life and everyone's. Amen.

No matter what I think or do, the universe knows.

No thought is unrecorded in the ethers of the universe. The Law of Cause and Effect insures that whatever I think will have an effect on some level. As a friend once said to me, "The universe keeps a perfect set of books." Today I seek right-minded thought, that only that which is right shall be returned to me.

I surrender my mind to the spirit of God, that my thoughts might be lifted to higher places. May I forgo blame and embrace blessing, forgo fear and embrace love, forgo violence and embrace peace. Thus may I become a co-creator with God.

Today I pray my mind become an instrument of love and a method of miracles. May my thoughts be guided by the thoughts of God, and turned into a blessing for myself and for all the world.

May my mind become an open door through which miracles can enter.

No miracle is too big or too complicated for God. It isn't limits to His power but only limits to my love that keep miracles from healing every problem in my life.

A loving thought opens a door, thus attracting a miracle. An unloving thought closes a door, thus deflecting one. May my mind be an open door through which miracles can flow freely into my life.

Life is simpler than I make it, for all things fall into only two categories: love or fear. Where I love, may I choose to love even more. Where I fear, may I choose the love and forgiveness that cast it out. I will thus experience my power to work miracles, through God's love that is in my mind.

I will not judge whom and what I cannot understand.

Often we have but a piece of information, a glimpse of someone's true being, and then still rush to judgment. Such temptation of the ego merely blinds us to truth and casts us into darkness. Only through the eyes of love can we truly see anything, and only through the Mind of Love can we truly understand.

I wish only to see what God would have me see. For there is love and yearning in everyone. May God give me new eyes that I might see and a new mind that I might understand.

Dear God,

May I not be tempted to think I know
What in fact I cannot know.
May I not be tempted to judge Your children
When You Yourself do not.
May my mind be free of the ego thoughts
That hide the light
In everyone.

Amen.

REFLECTION

On the Song of the Universe

The true you, your holy self, is beyond any limits of the mortal world. So are the talents and brilliance within you. When you dwell in that knowledge, simply recognizing and appreciating the divine spirit residing in all of us, you receive the charisma of a self-confident person.

Someone who has confidence in God comes across as confident to the world; someone who thinks of himself or herself as a follower of God comes across as a leader to the world. You'll develop a kind of invisible light, a sense of humble certitude, a greatness that comes from beyond yourself.

Your abilities, your intelligence, your talents, your personality, your circumstances, your dreams will all come together in a beautiful pattern. And you will see all this as your calling—a calling back and forth, in continuous song, from your heart to the universe and from the universe back to you.

May I learn to love as God loves.

Whom I do not like, God still loves. For God loves everyone. By turning away from love for anyone, I turn away from God. Today I choose not to counter His will, but to be His instrument.

I am an idea in the Mind of God. The Mind of God is the Mind of Love, for everyone and everything. Today may I learn to love as God loves, that I might learn who I really am.

Dear God,

Please lift my thoughts to love
For everyone and everything.
For then I will know what it means to love
And I will know who I really am.

Amen.

Today I replace my grievances with miracles.

The only sure way to rid myself of an enemy is to choose to be his friend. My withholding love from anyone is not what God would have me do.

Thus even someone who has been my enemy can miraculously become my friend. Today I allow the power of forgiveness to do for me what I cannot do. I pray for my enemy, despite my resistance, that he or she might become my friend.

Creating walls of separation between others and myself will never create a miracle. Love is the power that will defeat my enemy, by defeating within me any idea of having one. I choose to be rid of my enemies by choosing to love them instead. May my grievances dissolve, and miracles abound.

May my mind never be an instrument of attack.

While love would not always have me agree with a brother, it would always have me love him. May my mind be an arbiter of fairness, and never an instrument of attack.

In disagreeing with someone, may I do so with respect. In holding someone accountable, may I do so with honor. In setting a boundary, may I do so with love.

Dear God,

May my mind be a conduit of love
And not fear,
That I might somehow help
To heal this hurting world.
May my mind be clear
But my heart be always open,
According to Your will.

Amen.

I cleave to God, and to God only.

How often I cling to people or things, hoping that I can keep them close. In doing so, I repel the very people and things I love.

Today, may I cling only to God. As we depend on God within us, we become more independent people. Through the independence of my spirit, I attract everyone and everything that contributes to my good. Released from my ego, I free others to more easily love me.

Dear God,

Please remove
My attachment
To things that are not mine.
Remove my ego's grip
From the flow of all things good,
That all things good might flow through me.

Amen.

REFLECTION

On Internal Regreening

Some people wonder why the energy in their life seems not to be moving forward—when in fact the only thing holding them back is their own unwillingness to face the issues that still need to be faced, the shadows that still need to be owned, and the amends that still need to be made in order to free their energy and restart their engines. As long as we're stuck internally, our lives will be stuck externally; the only way to go wide in life is if we are willing to go deep. It doesn't matter if the problem happened decades ago; the challenge is to face it and deal with it now, so in the decades ahead you'll be released from the karmic trap of having always to reenact past disasters.

What sometimes seems as a slowing down of our jets is often anything but. Internal work is sometimes done more easily while sitting there thinking than while busily running around. A frantic schedule helps us to avoid taking a deeper look at ourselves, but at a certain point such avoidance simply does not and cannot work anymore. Slower lifestyles, candles and soft music in the house, yoga, meditation, and the like are often signs of an internal regreening. We are focusing on changes that support our deepening. And that deepening is the purpose of our lives.

Lost opportunities are
never truly lost.

I have not always behaved in ways that have maximized my opportunities. But the fact that I attracted them means that they were mine. Every lesson will come around again, and I will have a chance to learn it.

Through my atonement, humility, and sincere desire to get it right where I have gotten it wrong before, I will attract the same opportunities again in another form. God holds His miracles in trust for me until I am ready to receive them. He will send opportunities around again, with even bigger plans for how they can bless me and others now.

Dear God,

I am ready to learn what I did not learn before.
I am ready to grow and to be a better person
    because of what I know now.
I atone for the mistakes of my past
And pray that they be used miraculously
To create an even greater good.

Amen.

Being precedes doing, in me and in the world.

The only way I can know what I should be doing is to focus on who I should be. There are important things God would have me do, but I am responsible for becoming the vessel through which He can work. He can only work for me if I allow Him to work through me.

Putting my focus on who God would have me be, is the only sure way I will ever come close to discerning what He would have me do, and being able to do it. Being precedes doing, in me and in the world.

Dear God,

Please make me who You would have me be,
That I might do what You would have me do.
May I embody the love
And extend the peace
That alone can change the world.

Amen.

I pour light on any
troubling circumstance.

God disentangles any dysfunctional energy that pervades a situation, when I place it in His hands. In my mind's eye, I pour light on any troubling circumstance. I loosen my attitudinal grip. I will see it as a lesson in miracles, as God displays His infinite power to turn darkness into light.

I no longer hold on to the problem, for God Himself shall make it right. My emotional constriction does not serve. Expanding into the infinity of my being, relaxing into the arms of God, I approach the situation differently. And the situation will change.

Dear God,

I lay this problem on Your altar.
Please interpret this situation for me.
May I see only the love in others and in me.
Show me what I need to see,
Guide me to what I need to do.
Help me to forgive.
Raise me above the fear in my mind.
Thank you, God.

Amen.

REFLECTION

On Rebuilding Our Lives

No matter how broken or wounded we are, God will touch us in our broken places and heal us of our wounds. Today I look to God's strength to lift me up, though I have fallen and at times despair. There is no darkness His light does not dissolve, in me or in the world.

I base my identity on an eternal rock.

I do not look to the world for comfort; I look only to God. I do not look to the world for peace; I look only to God. I do not look to the world for security; I look only to God.

I base my identity on an eternal rock, no longer at the effect of a chaotic world. I seek love that lies beyond the world, that I might bring it here.

Dear God,

May Your spirit overshadow my mind
And give me eyes to see.
May I perceive the love I know exists
And overlook the rest.
May I rise above the darkness of the world
And my mind be bathed in light.
May I be calm and comforted
By truth.

Amen.

Today I choose to spread my wings.

I realize the huge calling of history at this time. We have been called to a collective genius, and each of us is being prepared to play our part. Our world needs spiritual giants, and it takes not ego but humility to sign up for the effort. Many of my problems arose because I chose to play small, thinking that there I would find safety.

But I was born with wings, and I'm meant to spread them. Anything less will hurt me, will deny love to myself and others, and will mean that I end my life never having flown the flight of spiritual glory.

Dear God,

If left to my own devices,
My perceptions will be skewed.
I surrender to You everything I think and feel.
Please take my past and plan my future.
Send Your spirit to redeem my mind,
That I might be set free.
May I be Your vessel
And serve the world.
May I become who You would have me be,
That I might do what You would have me do.

Amen.

REFLECTION

On Giving Up Old Stories

Even if your mother or father didn't tell you that you were wonderful when you were a child, your divine Father/Mother tells you that now. Spiritual understanding is a corrective to any false programming you might have received as a child. Rather than endlessly analyzing a tape from childhood, you can erase it by recording a new one. Spiritual growth involves giving up the stories of your past so the universe can write a new one. You are not denying your childhood; you are simply transcending any of its negative aspects.

God is your real Mother and God is your real Father. You are loved and adored and cared for and blessed. Accept that if even for a moment, and the torments of mortal childhood begin to pass away.

Prayer expresses my passion for God.

With my prayers I invite Him in, He who is already there. With prayer, I speak to God. With miracles, He responds. The endless chain of communication between loved and lover, between God and man, is the most beautiful song, the sweetest poem. It is the highest art and the most passionate love.

Dear God,

I give this day to You,
The fruit of my labor and the desires of my heart.
In Your hands I place all questions,
On Your shoulders I place all burdens.
I pray for my brothers and for myself.
May we return to love.
May we all be blessed.
May we find our way home,
From pain to peace,
From fear to love,
From hell to heaven.
For Thine is the Kingdom, and the Power,
*   and the Glory. Forever and ever.*

Amen.

I ask God to transform
all negative thoughts.

How do I quit the negative self-talk, the chronic repetition of thoughts and feelings that cause me to emotionally spiral downward? It's not always as easy as simply saying, "I won't think that way anymore." Entrenched thought forms are like a buildup of plaque on my consciousness. But I'm not asked to be my own transformer; I'm asked only to surrender the thoughts and feelings that need transforming. God will do the rest.

Dear God,

I feel myself falling into the hole
Of self-pity, self-obsession, and negativity.
I know I shouldn't think this way,
But I'm afraid and I cannot stop.
Please replace my thoughts with Yours, dear God.
I am willing to see myself and all things differently.
Please send me the miracle of new eyes and ears,
That I might know my greater good.

Amen.

REFLECTION

On Trusting Our Desires

Many people have a hard time allowing themselves to really want what they want. They think, at least sub-consciously, that asking for total happiness is asking for too much. They don't bother, therefore, to truly listen to their heart's desire.

But when your mind is attuned through prayer, meditation, and forgiveness; when your body is attuned through healthy nutrition and exercise; and when your behavior is attuned through a sincere effort at healthy living, then you've earned the right to trust yourself. When you're aligned with truth, your desires can be trusted. You have a knowing that they come from God.

I am divinely programmed to rise.

I am internally programmed to rise to my highest creative possibility. Nothing I do can erase the yearning of my soul to achieve it, or the yearning of the universe to give it to me. No deviation from love—on my part or anyone else's—can keep the universe from its divine intention that my life be one of fullness and joy.

According to *A Course in Miracles,* any miracle I might have deflected is "held in trust for you until you are ready to receive it." The universe has a built-in insurance policy. Whatever I have lost is programmed to return—in another form, in another situation, in another town, or with other people, perhaps, but through the power of atonement, it *will* return.

Dear God,

I feel that I have failed.
I feel that all my efforts have come to naught.
I feel shame at the way my life has turned out.
I do not know what to do or where to go.
Please, dear God, repair my heart,
Heal my mind, and change my life.
Pave a way for me out of darkness into light.
I atone for my errors, and I pray for forgiveness.
Please do for me what I cannot do.
Thank you, God.

Amen.

I surrender to God my work in the world.

To the ego mind, surrender means giving up. To the spiritual mind, surrender means giving in and receiving. Once I'm there, inside the holy place where all is inner riches, the outer gold of worldly prosperity appears in a miraculous way. It comes inviting me to use my wealth responsibly and to share it generously, as the universe so shared it with me.

As God so clothes the lilies in the field, He will surely clothe me. He asks that I extend to others the blessing and protection He has poured upon me, that His love might flow forth in an endless stream of miracles.

Dear God,

I surrender to You who I am, what I have, and what I do.
May my life and talents be used in whatever
    way serves You best.
I surrender to You my failures and any pain still in my heart.
I surrender to You my successes and the hopes that they contain.
May the light of Your love shine deep within my heart
And extend through me to bless the world.

Amen.

I dedicate my talents to God.

That which is proactively placed in the service of love is protected from the grips of fear. That which is proactively placed in the service of deep sanity is protected from the grips of neurosis. That which is proactively placed in the service of what is good, holy, and beautiful is protected from the forces of destruction.

Today, I take myself, my work, and the God within me seriously—dedicate myself daily, hourly, even moment by moment to love's purposes—and the ego won't have a chance. It knows a holy mind when it sees one.

Dear God,

I dedicate to You my talents and abilities.
May they be used in a way that serves Your purposes.
I surrender to You my business and finances.
May my work be lifted to its highest possibility,
As a blessing on all the world.

Amen.

REFLECTION

On the Miracle of Forgiveness

It's fairly easy to stay loving and serene when others always act the way you want them to, but that's not a realistic picture of life. Everyone's imperfect, everyone's wounded, and most of us have been somewhat scathed at one time or another by the casual cruelty of others.

Forgiveness involves faith in a love that's greater than hatred, and a willingness to see the light in someone's soul even when their personality harbors darkness. Forgiveness doesn't mean that someone didn't act horribly; it simply means that we choose not to focus on their guilt. In focusing on it, we make it real to us, and in making it real to us, we make it real *for* us. The only way to deliver ourselves from vulnerability to other people's behavior is by identifying with the part of them that lies beyond their bodies. We can look beyond others' behavior to the innocence in their souls. In doing so, we not only free *them* from the weight of our condemnation, but we free ourselves as well.

That is the miracle of forgiveness.

The power to work miracles
is my natural inheritance.

As a child of God, I am entitled to the riches my Father bestows on me: the miracles that occur when my mind is attuned to love.

In remembering who He is, and who I am, I remember the power within me. This is not a power to merely fix things. It is the power to transform the world. May I use my power with magnanimity and grace, to work miracles wherever I am.

Dear God,

I receive the gift You have bestowed on me
To work miracles on Your behalf.
May my mind so serve Your purposes
That in time we come to co-create
A heaven here on earth.
And so it is.

Amen.

ACKNOWLEDGMENTS

Thanks to all the marvelous people who helped me put this book together. It was a sweet, meaningful experience bringing all our hearts and creative talents to the effort.

My abiding thanks to ...

Mickey Maudlin, for steering my literary ship with calm and creativity. I'm very grateful for the opportunity to deliver my words into such capable hands.

Ellis Levine, for literary counsel, constant back-and-forths, and always-sage advice.

Tammy Vogsland, for keeping my material world in right order. And that is no joke.

Kathryn Renz, Lisa Zuniga, Terri Leonard, and Michele Wetherbee, for all their excellence in taking a manuscript and turning it into a book; and Claudia Boutote, Laina Adler, Amy VanLangen, and Melinda Mullin, for letting the world know about it. Also, Jeremy Cowart and David Kaufman, for the beauty they brought to the process.

Mark Tauber, for publishing my work. Thank you for the honor.

Lesley Silverman, for generous and impeccable assistance with the manuscript. It's a better book because you were at my side.

Frances Fisher, Wendy Zahler, and David Kessler, for the blessings of friendship. I cannot thank you enough.

India Williamson, for being the daughter of my dreams.

To all of you, my abiding gratitude. This book carries your love, as well as mine, out into the world.

Explore Other

—— *Marianne Williamson Classics* ——

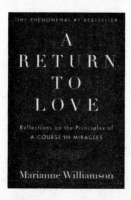

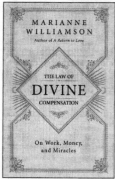

HarperOne
An Imprint of HarperCollins*Publishers*